A trilogy
by Yannis Andricopoulos

In Bed with Madness

The Greek Inheritance

The Future of the Past

Copyright © Yannis Andricopoulos, 2008

The moral rights of the author has been asserted
No part of any contribution may be reproduced in any form
without permission, except for the quotation of brief passages
in criticism and discussion.

Published in the UK by Imprint Academic
PO Box 200, Exeter EX5 5HY, UK

Published in the USA by Imprint Academic
Philosophy Documentation Center
PO Box 7147, Charlottesville, VA 22906-7147, USA

ISBN 978-1845401313

A CIP catalogue record for this book is available from the
British Library and US Library of Congress

www.imprint-academic.com

Yannis Andricopoulos

The Future of the Past

From the Culture of Profit to the Culture of Joy

Contents

Back to the Greeks   5

Part I: Absent Certainties

1. Weight or Lightness?   19
2. A View from Nowhere   29
3. Elusive but not Extant   39
4. Battle for Your Own Sake   47

Part II: Looking Inwards

1. From Postmodern to Postmortem   55

Part III: Spring Depends on Us

1. An Unnameable Essence   71
2. Contradictions Are Our Hope   81
3. The Unfinished Business   86
4. The Unsubmissive   94
5. Good, But Not Good Enough   104
6. Beyond the Price of Sausages   109
7. The Market or the Citizens   114
8. Virtue and Guts   126
9. An Ethical Holism   136
10. Some 'Normal' Assumptions   143
11. Perfect in its Vagueness   148
12. The 'Right Thing'   157

Part IV Epilogue

The Education of Desire   171

Index   177

Part I: Back to the Greeks

The humanistic world of the Greeks, so audaciously innocent, hit the rocks of the rigid, formalised, hierarchical, exclusive, intolerant, aphilosophical and also gloomy religiosity of Judaism, Christianity and later of Islam. 'Out-distanced and out-invented' as Philip Larkin might have said, the Greeks were overtaken by time which had gone ahead without them. The world had outlived its dreams; the fire had gone; the birds forgot how to fly. 'O mind, great charioteer', Kazantzakis sadly reflected, 'you hold the myriad reins of sacred virtue and of shame, of fear, of hope in your strong hands and drive on towards the plunging cliff'. History in the centuries that followed was made by those who, as Byron said, 'butcher'd half the earth, and bullied t'other'. As depressingly, Edward Gibbon, the English historian, concluded: 'history is little more than the register of crimes, follies, and misfortunes of mankind'.

The greatest crimes against humanity since the good old days, before polygamy became a sin, were committed in the name of Christianity, and then socialism, nationalism, freedom, civilisation or progress. Humanitarian bombing and savage military campaigns in the name of Tony Blair's 'liberal imperialism' is the latest, blessed, as one can safely assume, by God Himself. God, as a Methodist minister elucidated for the benefit of mankind during the US imperialist war against the Spanish in Cuba and the Philippines in 1898, had chosen 'the Anglo-Saxons to conquer the world for Christ by dispossessing feeble races, and assimilating and moulding others'. The mass graves on the banks of the moaning rivers of history look as if they can hardly take one more word from another worthy truth, 'liberal imperialist' or otherwise.

Ignominiously, the universal truths of both Christianity and modernism also produced definitions of the 'essential' in human nature, culture and institutions which only stereotyped, homogenised, marginalised, dominated, oppressed and excluded human beings. Women were created not for the pen, but for the needle, and children were to be seen but not heard. Christianity denied the body – Plotinus, the third century A.D. founder of Neoplatonism, is best remembered for saying that he 'blushed because he had a body'; and 'the royal race' denied the 'blacks' and the 'yellows' membership of the human race. For capitalism, the poor existed only to make the rich richer – 'the seed ye sow, another reaps', Shelley cried with rhythmical rage, 'the wealth ye find, another keeps, the robes ye weave, another wears, the rams ye forge, another bears'. Inhaling memories even from the not-so-distant past, when with a hundred drachmas you could buy a mule, with ten a woman, does not inebriate one with pride.

Modernisation, which like gravity can be resisted but only for so long, and its merciless pursuit of material expansion, euphemistically called 'Growth', although of West European origins, turned into a spatially and temporally neutralised model for all processes of social development. Operating behind the veil of manipulative language, it fostered domination and exploitation, and crushed the otherness of the Other. Simultaneously leading, as German sociologist Max Weber said, to the rationalisation and disenchantment of the world, it subjugated everything, nature, society, individuality, philosophy, art and language, to its homogenising drive. It separated human nature from nature and psychologically distorted the human psyche. For Horkheimer and Adorno, the Frankfurt School thinkers, this was 'nature's revenge'.

'Progress' brought more comfort to those who have plenty of it. But, like old age, it did not come by itself. It brought along dangers – climate change, wars which can destroy the entire planet, growing inequalities, fundamentalism and terrorism – all of which transcend national frontiers. It forced us to live on a diet of carbon dioxide, commute sometimes for hours in crowded trains, spend the day in the physical and mental prison of offices though the latter may sometimes be as spacious as the bridge of the Starship Enterprise, and seek escape in the bizarre world of the TV. It taught us to live in fear of being mugged, avoid talking to 'strangers', make the most out of the tasteless food stored in our deep freezer, watch, impotently, the slaughter in Iraq's abattoir, and go to bed thinking of the next day's sales. Thankfully, though the alienating and self-alienating process has been accelerated, smiling has not as yet been criminalised and a 'hello' to the neighbours is still free of charge.

Like Medusa, the free market, together with globalisation, seems to have succeeded in turning men to stone with its gaze; or, in this instance, turning a community of humans into a community of providers and consumers. Any new systems which emerge in society, Jürgen Habermas stressed, become increasingly detached from the social structures and develop at the expense of their links with the whole. Real life becomes more and more provincial, shrinks to a subsystem whose only function is to ensure the functionality of the system. Humans do not matter.

This is the madness answering to the name of Reason, truth or progress, all illogical components, as sociologist Vilfredo Pareto held, of ideologies manipulated by élites in their own interests – his insights did not help him all that much as in 1923 he backed Mussolini in the hope that he would restore the missing order. Madness and non-madness, reason and non-reason, Michel Foucault said, are inextricably involved: inseparable at the moment when they do not yet exist, and existing for each other, in relation to each other, in the exchange which separates them.

Meanwhile, there is nothing, not even a rough, yet credible alternative to the current structures of this mad system which, as a poster in a London's May demo so charmingly suggested 'should be replaced by something nicer'. Perhaps, life is too complicated for anything else, or, as Neo-Freudian psychiatrist Karen Horney put it, madness is a lubricant that keeps the world spinning. Hence the inability to suggest a simple solution to the growing problems – simple solutions, those recommended by fundamentalists, are in any case unable by definition to provide a good answer. Indeed, the greater the do-gooders' zeal, as Socrates said, the greater the danger they pose.

Looking for inspiration in the search for a viable alternative, in *The Greek Inheritance* I went far back to the roots of our Western culture, the eternal world of the Greeks. The twentieth century and its modernist solidities answering to the name of colonialism, imperialism, nationalism, Fascism, communism and anti-communism, progress, material growth and democracy, always half-baked, had, just like the theological solidities of the past, swept away the humanistic, democratic culture of Greece. So did the anti-humanist postmodernist critique and the politically-correct approaches of the last few decades of the twentieth century which in the name of diversity – 'Hey Ho, Hey Ho, Western Culture's Got to Go' – marginalised Europe and her culture. The journey to a location that was off the world's philosophical tourist map was rather lonely.

But as the old turgid certainties have gone, postmodernism's freedom to be has been compromised by the ensuing intellectual disorientation, the free market has triumphed to the discomfort, even embarrassment, of many of its beneficiaries, and the fundamentalist threat, a threat to civilisation itself, has raised its ugly head. Eyes are once again turning to Greece, for, as Sorbonne professor Marcel Conche put it, the Greek past is the only future worth fighting for.

Non-European cultures need, naturally, to be respected. They deserve to be respected as the universalisation of European culture under the banner of development has led to the cultural colonisation of the world and the alienation of entire cultures from their heritage and social systems. But equally true, regard for the precious European inheritance of human and political rights and for Europe's magnificent culture cannot be dismissed as 'Eurocentric'. Nor can Greece's culture at the very heart of it. 'At the beginning of everything we know', as Alfred North Whitehead, the English philosopher, said, Greece is, in any case, still very much with us.

Her values are still strolling through Europe's lightbewitched alleys, facing eternity in the multitudinous classical allusions found everywhere, and cradled in the thoughts of each new generation. Her essential secularism, searching culture, open society and democratic institutions are at the foundation of our own world, in the chromosomes of western civilisation – 'we are all Greeks', P.B. Shelley exclaimed, 'our laws, our literature, our religion, our arts, they all have their root in Greece'. In her we find the roots of our science, literature, philosophy, sports and politics, of our heroes, myths and nymphs. Her exclusions, boundaries and demarcations that were set in classical Athens, Michael Kustow, the film producer, writer and broadcaster, said, 'have become a kind of DNA code of our culture'. They have cast their spell over two thousand five hundred years of Western thinking. Greece's eternally youthful culture is the West's spiritual home, the foundation of its culture, the springs of its wisdom.

Her spirit, invisible and unconquerable, i.e. the human spirit that, as Socrates said, makes the soul of any creature absolutely fearless and indomitable, together with the universalism of Greek philosophy and culture have eliminated the ages. They have ensured that, rather than 'a clanging of bells lost in the mist', Greece will never fade into the darkness of the aeons. 'When a truth', the 'Greek' nineteenth century American poet and essayist Ralph Waldo Emerson said, 'that fires the soul of Pindar fires mine, time is no more'. Refreshing itself in the springs of Greek wisdom, the world can win back some of the much needed inspiration in the battle against both monotheistic fundamentalism and the free market's latria of profit.

Free from the oppression of monolithic theocratic solidities, the original and, perhaps because of it, honest face of our world, the Greek culture gave man the freedom to be himself. The resulting civilisation, the 'miracle' which is 'so surpassing or so difficult to account', as Bertrand Russell pointed out, has simply been incomparable to anything else. The 'miracle', which is at the root of everything we know, was the liberation of the human race from fear of the unknown. Reverence of, or submission to, the mysteries of the physically or metaphysically impenetrable had given way to critical thinking. The world had only to be understood and rationally explained.

Rather than stand in the way and give the Greeks a list of prohibitions, the Olympian Gods, the Greeks' senior brothers, were only too happy to sanction the unlimited development of human potential. Unlike the tyrants of the monotheistic religions, they had no need to be revered, feared and obeyed. Rather than 'slaves of the Lord', the Greeks were proud to be humans, masters of their own fate, utterly confident in their own power, indeed intoxicated by it, inquisitive and fearless. They thus crossed, the horizon line as if they were Gods themselves. Human law was made by humans alone. Life was theirs, not their Gods. The amorality of divine omnipotence could not impair the dignity of man. It could not damage the Greeks' moral framework that no other society has been able to emulate, either. In a world still split between the free and joyous spirit of the Greeks and that of repressive theocratic systems, Greece remains the departure point for any secular society with a divinely human presence.

Hence the search for a visionary consciousness inspired by the Greeks, the adulation of Greece, which is evident in the work of so many thinkers as diverse as Marx and Nietzsche, Marcuse and Heidegger, Shakespeare and Joyce, Beethoven and Wagner, Shelley and Ezra Pound, all members of the non-religious opposition to the distortion of Greek values by the heirs of the Enlightenment.

The same culture of joy is the beacon of any society determined to resist the degrading capitalist culture of profit, the guide to sanity's shores. Greece's rationalism honoured the free human spirit rather than the logic of the merchants, her morality was a celebration of Justice rather than of sexual deprivation, and her unforced commitment to human values gave man his dignity. Infused with the same ethicality, the holism of the Greeks acknowledged nature as 'us' rather than the Other, honoured the whole person – spirit, mind and flesh, and produced an education system designed to bring up youngsters as exceptional human beings and citizens rather than as functionaries of the system. Their sense of beauty over utility, the beauty of forms and of the mind, of institutions, laws and sciences, or of the virtues of temperance and Justice, 'walking through the earth', as Rilke would say, 'like a young year', and their democracy, are still humanity's guiding spirit.

These cardinal points of reference are the educated memory's guide through the labyrinthine complexities of our time, the inspiration in the journey towards the realisation of all human potentials in both freedom and also responsibility towards the community and our environment. Hence, as Friedrich Schiller said, the Greeks are 'our rivals, nay, frequently our models'. The same sentiments were expressed by Georg Hegel for whom the Greeks 'are our models in all that is great, beautiful, noble and free'. Their achievements, Friedrich Nietzsche, likewise, urged in his 'monumentalistic' mood, rather than being a symbol of an irretrievable past, are, instead, a challenge and a promise. In spite of the onslaught on the Enlightenment by modernism and also by the Romantic, theological, existentialist or postmodernist opposition to them, the values of the classical tradition, in Goethe's words, 'the strong, fresh, gay, and healthy' holistic culture of the Greeks were, thus, never lost.

Of course, as young Marx regretfully concluded when talking about the impossibility of reinstating the virtues of the ancient world, we cannot return to the past. Many things cannot change. Mountains do not grow. The revival of the city-state, which would or could fully and actively involve its citizens in its running, is unattainable. So is the territorially-based nationally-bound 'society', the 'blood and soil' entities linked with common roots and a separate identity. Society and national state have been replaced respectively by cosmopolitanism and globalism in the context of which even the concept of 'social' appears to be historically outdated. As it is, national, economic and social entities cannot, therefore, effectively resist their integration into the world market and its social model or even protect their own culture and identity. Even Europe as a whole, faced with mass immigration which will further and dramatically alter its demographics, may well not be able to hold on to her traditions. In any case, however noble, no dream can guarantee deliverance or hold the promise of coming grace.

But if, in times of infirmity, one needs to open the book of memory and look back for inspiration, the eyes turn, as Shelley said, to 'the wondrous fame of the past world, the vital words and deeds of minds whom neither time nor change can tame'. No 'past world' other than that of Greece can provide such an inspiration.

I touched it, tasted it, smelled it myself, not in Athens, but in Paris during the joyous spring of 1968, the 'revolution' which broke out like a festival of life, and made sure that nothing could keep 'shut the windows of the sky'. Going beyond all known boundaries, people questioned everything, from sexuality to work, if work meant we turn into parts of a soulless, mechanical process that has no human meaning. They defied authority because authority rests on manipulation and coercion to the benefit of those in power; opposed domination and exploitation no longer identified with strictly defined class interpretations; and rejected a culture geared to satisfying consumer needs while killing the spirit of man. In the spring of '68, when Aphrodite, followed by doves and sparrows and swathed in flowers which sprang from the soil wherever she trod, modernism was incisively confronted and the post-war conservative consensus broken.

The revolt against our culture, because that is what it was, placed its trust in the creativity and imagination of the individual. It gave people the confidence to challenge the 'establishment', claim the future for themselves, be the architects of their own fate. Everything seemed possible – except, perhaps, changing sex every year. The world had been restored to youth like Phaon, the lover of Sappho. It was offered in an oyster to the young, the uncontaminated. The dream did, of course, end, but the 'revolution', the unfinished revolution as novelist and cultural theorist Joan Smith rightly called it in her book *Moralities*, full of potential, remains the source of our inspiration. The memory it left, which French president Nicolas Sarkozy wants to 'liquidate', is still with us like the curve of that beautiful body in bed, the scent of the spring, the brilliance and gaiety of a Matisse painting. And memory is wealth. 'I remember, therefore I possess', as Yannis Ritsos put it in his usual concinnity which gives such distinction to his style.

Having survived the long Christian winter and rediscovered in the fifteenth century, the spirit of Greece invaded Europe's psyche. 'The idols', Roberto Calasso, the Italian contemporary writer, stated lyrically, 'were back at last'. Herman Broch, that great twentieth century German novelist who like Proust and Joyce entertained in his novels both poetry and philosophy, could have, 'in spite of his horror of being indiscreet', asked again 'where (they) had been all this time'. The vision of three major German figures – the brilliant art historian J.J. Winckelmann, who was murdered in Trieste in 1768, the Homeric scholar F.G.A. Wolff, and the enlightened Prussian bureaucrat Wilhelm von Humboldt, on whose ideas the *Humboldt-Universität zu Berlin* was founded in 1810 - was at the very foundation of the new Hellenism that captured the soul of so many German giants.

Goethe, who, as Ritsos might have said, 'touched the lips of immortality with his thumb', fully endorsed the Greek holistic, rational understandings, including its sensuousness and also 'pantheism', i.e. the immanence of God in everything. Beethoven, likewise, thought of God as a presence in our living whole, 'in a purely earthly, blissfully earthly consciousness'. Schiller, for his part, striving for the liberation of sensuality which would, he believed, lead both to a universal gratification and the gratification of the free individual, envisaged an 'Elysian age', an age in which people would be able to live in harmony with their world as in the 'Arcadian age', the age of Greece. Hölderlin, the unreconstructed Jacobin, who, like Nietzsche, felt like a Greek himself, called for a total renewal so that 'pleasure becomes serious and work a joy'. Capturing a dream and then re-dreaming it, Hölderlin committed himself, just like William Blake and Shelley, to the 'forthcoming revolution of attitudes'.

More political than Hölderlin, Blake, however, went further and castigated the capitalist 'oppressors of Albion' and the 'dishonest' Methodist and Evangelist interpreters of the Bible. Their 'vision of Christ', he wrote in *The Everlasting Gospel*, was his own vision's 'greatest Enemy'. Torn throughout his life between rational deism and mystic apocalyptic visions, Blake opted eventually for the former when he reaffirmed the joy of sexuality.

The movement for the return to the classics, which reached its apogee in England during the Victorian era, owes a huge debt to Byron, the poet known also for his dismissal of the Christian Church, his enthusiasm for the French Revolution, to which the British, including the Romantics Coleridge, Wordsworth and Southey, objected violently, and his contempt for the scramble for power, the riches and the hypocrisy of his own class. None of this endeared him to the British establishment. The Church, on the other hand, could not forgive a 'man who outraged the laws of our Divine Lord', as Bishop Ryle wrote in 1924. Though comparable only to Goethe in nineteenth century Europe, Byron, who died in 1824 as a soldier during Greece's struggle for independence, was not, thus, accepted for burial at Westminster Abbey – this happened only in 1969. The feeling was reciprocated, for as he wrote, the thought that his bones might rest in England would be enough to 'drive me mad on my death-bed ... I would not even feed her worms if I could help it'.

Shelley, another child of the Enlightenment and almost as appreciative of the Greek classical tradition as Byron, was, on the other hand, a committed socialist, the revolutionary who called the 'Men of England' to 'rise like lions after slumber ... shake your chains to earth like dew ... ye are many – they are few'.

Modernist Reason, this walking calculation and abstraction, was most seriously challenged by Immanuel Kant, the only philosopher who shared the status of Plato and Aristotle. As opposed to Heidegger or Bookchin, who challenged modernity from the Presocratic point of view, Kant, however, anchored his philosophy in the humanistic movement of the Stoics. He rejected both Reason and its cold dictates, by appealing to the heart, and bridged the dichotomy between Reason and intuition, senses and intellect, desire and cognition by a third faculty of an aesthetic nature, which he called judgment. Judgment strengthened sensuousness against the tyranny of Reason. The Romantics, those who, guided by an 'inner light', were attempting to bypass the critical tribunal of the faculties and interpret the world by intuition, encountered only his scorn; and the Christian God had no place in his thinking – he believed, instead, in an immanent God, present throughout the universe. Hence Frederick William II of Prussia ordered him neither to teach nor write on religious subjects.

Kant reaffirmed the humanistic values of the Stoics, the 'inalienable' human rights, 'sacred', irrespective of costs to the 'ruling powers'. Despite his moving belief in the destiny of man, by comparison to the Presocratics, he was, however, on the conservative side. Greek radicalism did not appeal to him. His thesis that every human being is an end in itself was noble enough in the age of industrialism when man had become a means to an end, which was capitalist growth. But for the Greeks, man was not the supreme end in a way which could legitimise the degradation of nature and the world into mere means to human ends. Likewise, Kant's autonomy of the subject manifested itself in the individual's relations to the self; yet, for the Greeks, the individual's relation to society and social justice and the city-state and democracy were as essential. Kant further rejected the principle of pleasure, which for the Greeks was essential, and placed moral virtue and obedience to a moral law above intellect, feeling and body. For the Greeks there was no hierarchy – in the context of *areté*, always seen in holistic terms, they were all equally valued.

Unlike Kant's, Hegel's own philosophy was anchored in the Presocratic perception of the world as one complex organism, the whole, an 'absolute' infused with a cosmic spirit, *Geist*, governed by Reason, 'the sovereign of the world'. The same mystical whole is subject to Heraclitus' doctrine of change – rather than being, it is perpetually becoming, and, like the human body, has no independent parts. Each part is an aspect of the whole, its position being determined by its relation to the whole. Irreligiously, Hegel, like Plethon, contrasted Christianity with ancient Greece, which he idealised, and proposed a new 'folk religion that does not force its teachings upon anyone, nor does violence to any human conscience'. His dismissal of Christianity, this 'inhumane' religion, was endorsed by Ludwig Andreas Feuerbach, the philosopher of humanity as he became known, who extolled the merits of polytheism, and argued that man could realise his essence if he replaced faith in God by faith in man.

Hegel's 'dialectical triad' – thesis, antithesis, synthesis – was adopted by Marx, but not in its mystified form. Idealism was transformed into a dialectical materialism which applied Hegel's dialectics to an existing material reality governed by natural laws, independent from consciousness and epistemologically explained. Marx accepted, too, Hegel's notion of the whole, except that this whole, a causally interconnected totality, unified, contradictory and perpetually evolving, was free from quasi-mystical world views. On these grounds Marx stretched his arms out to grasp the future, the 'inevitable' and yet elusive communist society, features of which were intended to be in tune with the humanistic culture of Greece. His imagination was captivated, in particular, by the ethos of the Greek polis and the insistence on *areté*, the all-round development of the individual, which the Marxist positivist orthodoxy and its 'heroic' march into the future never bothered to consider.

Nietzsche, likewise, looked back to the Greeks, those immortal mortals, for inspiration to recover their superb spirit, for things were lamentably 'human, only too human'. Man had killed 'God'. 'I seek God, I seek God', cries his madman, who on a bright morning lit a lantern and, just like Diogenes who was looking for a 'just' man, ran to the marketplace. 'Where is God gone? ... We have killed him, you and I! We are all his murderers ... God is dead! God remains dead! And we have killed him'. We did so again one hundred years later when Christ, in a Volkswagen advertisement, banned and therefore never seen on our screens, invited his friends in the Last Supper to 'rejoice because a new Golf had been born'.

For someone, like Nietzsche, who had stressed that his roots were firmly in the French Enlightenment and the Greek tradition, the announcement of his madman was not a rejection of Reason itself but of its interpretation in the new era of modernity. Hence his view that there are no facts, but only interpretations and evaluations, which, as it happens, are fundamentally flawed, his rejection of morality and its rational foundation, his repudiation of religion and all petrified views of the past which create hardened stereotypes. As Rilke, the great German poet who shared Nietzsche's views, said, 'we are not reliably at home in the interpreted world'. The rational foundation of morality, Nietzsche said just as the postmodernists did later, rests on the concept of a universal morality which does not exist, for no moral code can be unconditionally applied to all men. The world's interplay of forces has no inherent structure nor final end.

To escape from the 'interpreted world', the German philosopher did not seek consolation in the otherworldliness of most of the Romantics, but in the nobility of Greece, the joyous, Dionysian affirmation of life as sought by Zarathustra in his 'Drunken Song'. The Dionysian 'eternal joy of existence' was counterbalanced, however, by the Apollonian, the civilising impulse, which embodies the concept of order. The ideal, perceived in naturalistic terms, was a human being with exceptional features, independent and creative, reaching towards the attainment of a 'higher humanity'. The man whom Nietzsche's madness celebrated so brilliantly is the sane, balanced man of the ancient world, the one who combines sensuousness and spirituality, feeling and intellect, sense and passion. As always, the clamour for the confinement of Reason, the killer, is raised in the cells of madness, the temples of Reason's worship, rather than in sanity's cathedrals.

The opposition to the distortion of the Enlightenment's values was carried on by the German sociologist Max Weber, who drew upon the Greek humanistic ideals in his critique of his overly rationalised society, and Martin Heidegger. Our tragedy, the latter stated, consists in 'the oblivion of Being', 'Being' originally in Greek philosophy designating our 'spiritual destiny' to which we cannot find our way back. Firmly rooted in the Greek philosophical tradition, his thesis decisively influenced many other major thinkers, including several contemporary American political theorists and before them Hannah Arendt, one of the most original political theorists of the twentieth century, and Herbert Marcuse, the intellectual force behind the French May of '68.

Arendt's vision of politics as the means to the individual's self-realisation and self-actualisation, expounded in *The Human Condition*, was fully inspired by the Greek vision. Politics, not in its current degraded version, but in its Greek form, a genuine good, an end in itself, she held, enabled the Greeks to 'reveal actively their unique personal identities and thus make their appearance in the human world'. The public realm provided the place where human beings could rise above the drudgery and the banalities of everyday life, au pairs and loyalty cards, property ladders and air fresheners, burst the chains of necessity and achieve greatness, the only criterion of action. Except that necessity, as Milan Kundera said, is heavy, and only what is heavy is valued. And greatness in our days, Kazantzakis had concluded earlier, is to live without hope.

Advancing the Greek model as the source of inspiration can, however, be as complicated as the attempt to work out 'objectively' the meaning and the purpose of life.

Part II: Absent Certainties
1. Weight or Lightness?

A commonly shared vision requires a return to universally shared values which the western intellectual élite has in the last quarter of the twentieth century decisively turned its back on. Considering what visions have done to us both in the distant and the recent past but also in the present, this is fully understandable. But considering also what the absence of any sense of common purpose is doing to us now, it is fully incomprehensible. Yet a common vision seems to be beyond our reach. In the postmodernist realm, a world which has blunted both our capacity for wonder and our ability to tell 'objectively' right from wrong, we do not know what is worth pursuing for the benefit of us all. We cannot tell, as Milan Kundera, the novelist, put it, what is positive, 'weight or lightness'.

'The key', as Yeats would have it, is then 'turned on our uncertainty'. We twin the doubt, which is unable to excuse itself for its sophistication, and become one with a confusion enchanted by its nescience. The inhabitants of the small Greek island of Siphnos, Herodotus tells us, used to share out, each year, the proceeds of their gold and silver mines. They seemed to have no doubt as to what is good and right. We do.

No issue is, of course, straightforward. The size of the world depends on where you live. To decide whether thrift, marriage, consumer society, hot speech graphics, individualism, hunting or the sublime, in the old sense, are good or bad, we need a criterion, and this criterion, particularly in times of transition, is not given. Nobody apart from those of uncontrollable urges, i.e. the self-appointed guardians of disesteemed values, can give us an estimate of virtue. Even sin is indefinable because it does not come without a self-propelled mechanism of seductive promises and frolicsome excuses.

As it is, nothing can look bad to everybody by definition. After all even Nero had his admirers – and fresh violets on his grave.

Life may be intrinsically valuable, yet there are many who argue convincingly enough that, given their uniqueness, equally valuable are works of art, cultures, languages and natural species. One cannot easily measure one good thing against another. Bellerophon, grandson of Sisyphus, advanced on foot against Iobates' palace supported by Poseidon's great waves rolling slowly forward, and no man could persuade him to stop. Could the women? They hoisted their skirts to the waist and offered themselves to him one and all, if only he would relent. I will not tell you the end of the story – it is probably enough to know that Bellerophon was a very decent man. But the story itself does raise an ethical issue unresolved, perhaps, to this day.

Likewise, human life is 'sacred', yet issues such as abortion, euthanasia or capital punishment split the West down the middle. So do issues relating to drugs, pornography, genetically modified food or renewable sources of energy. Disagreements cover, indeed, the entire spectrum of human activities. Homosexuality may be celebrated in Sydney and Los Angeles and frowned upon in Cairo and Moscow. The homogenisation of the world's culture may be welcomed as it obliterates narrow-minded old divisions or hated as it destroys what took people millennia to build. Europe's frontiers should be wide open to Third World economic refugees because her population is ageing or remain tightly closed because she will, otherwise, forfeit her identity. There is no objective criterion on the strength of which we can definitely decide what is right and what is wrong.

After all, the world is full of people who belong to different centuries; and one cannot disengage principles from understandings deriving from history or from the meaning they take when interpreted in terms of national, traditional, religious, class, race, gender and other identity interests. Keiko, the beautiful Hiroshima survivor disfigured by the atomic explosion and brought to America by some Manhattan liberals to articulate the horrors of the bomb in Shaena

Lambert's absorbing novel *Radiance*, was an innocent war victim but not for everybody. There were also those who viewed her as a manipulated propaganda tool or a reminder of Japanese war cruelty. What looks good to 'us' does not look as good to 'them'. Herodotus makes the point humorously and compellingly. If all mankind, he says, agreed to meet, and everyone brought his own faults along with him for the purpose of exchanging them for somebody else's, there is not a man who, after taking a good look at his neighbour's faults, would not be only too happy to return home with his own.

Blair and Bush's comforting vision of a simple, eternal, universally accepted version of values, advanced from the heights of their moral self-righteousness, rests, therefore, on their purposefully misreading the picture. Voting is not everything. Time and again, people have sacrificed political freedom for the sake of freedom from foreign domination or in the cause of greater security and order. Many value the fundamental moral laws as laid down by their God or their conscience much more than the benefits of the free market, while white Americans have for most of their history placed the dominance of their racial community above any universal right to freedom. Speaking on behalf of universal values to which the entire world should adhere is often nothing more than the manifestation of another form of fundamentalism associated with national messianism. The defence of human rights on a global scale, to which the US commits itself only very selectively, has nothing to do with what comes with their assertion, i.e., the projection of its 'superior' liberal capitalist model, its own cultural values and its narrow national interests. Rather than an end in itself, democracy and human rights have become an instrument of national power.

Trying to validate substantive principles particularly across different contexts and cultures is a near impossibility. Evaluations, socially constructed, cannot transcend one's own cultural context – the 'acontextual evaluation' which anthropologist Ernest Gellner said we need in order to assess fully a cultural phenomenon is unobtainable.

We are all defined by our own histories and value systems, by customs, opinions, prejudices and fears. Hence the Sophists' refusal to answer the question what is Justice – the only question which would make sense for them was what is Justice in Miletus or Corinth. This may be good as far as it goes, but as Blaise Pascal, the seventeenth century philosopher, said, Justice, whose limits are marked by a river, 'true on this side of the Pyrenees, false on the other, is a funny sort of justice'. Moral concepts do inexorably clash often so violently that even murder can in certain circumstances be seen as a morally legitimate course of action, inhumanly taking precedence over human law. 'The killing by a Jew of a non-Jew under any circumstances is not regarded as murder', Jewish fundamentalists claim, invoking the Halacha, the Jewish law based on the Talmud. Even the abominable murder of Israeli Prime Minister Yitzak Rabin was hailed by them as the fulfilment of an obligation under Talmudic law. Men, Blaise Pascal again reflected, never do evil so completely and cheerfully as when they do it from religious conviction.

An impartial determination of goodness, involving detachment from our perspectives, absolute objectivity, dispassionate views, is as unattainable as universal fair weather. The lines separating a pragmatic discourse, which defines what is useful, from an ethical discourse, which delineates the good irrespective of individual preferences, and, finally, from a moral discourse, which describes the good from the point of view of its universality, are blurred. Ethical concerns do not rest on consensus. The concept of goodness has no independent properties on the strength of which we can define it. This is not, of course, the exclusive property of our age, an age charitable to its burnt-out passions, oblivious to its decrepitudes and impervious to circumspection. Women had to commit suicide on the death of their husbands in prehistoric Greece, yet Gorgophone, Perseus' daughter, rather than follow the custom chose to remarry. What a social schism this must have provoked in her time!

The fundamental and perennial question, first posed by Socrates, as to how one should live, what constitutes a good life, cannot, thus, be objectively answered. Parents can teach their offspring to seek success rather than happiness, to value rights rather than obligations, to treat people respectfully or not, to care or not to care, to look forward to an easy as opposed to a demanding time, to pursue petty interests or lead a just and honourable life. But it is all arbitrary. The language of morals is arbitrary. No objective criteria or understandings, shared values or generally accepted standards exist to guide us. Rain is objectively wet both here and in Syria, or, as Demosthenes said, sons are dearer to man than nephews, but the lifestyle of Michael Jackson has nothing objectively good or bad about it. Likewise, the United States has been happy to spend $2 billion a week to fight the war in Iraq, but is reluctant to spend less than 0.1 per cent of that amount to save the lives of tens of millions in Africa. Such a policy may well be 'morally repugnant' as, indeed, a deputy executive director of Unicef described it. But his view is not as unquestionable as the statement that lightning is faster than a tortoise.

Rational consensus in a discourse which tries to determine one's course of action pragmatically, ethically and morally seems impossible to achieve. As John Rawls, the American philosopher, author of *A Theory of Justice*, acknowledged, irrespective of its conception in terms of impartiality and neutrality, the right and the good is never going to be free from substantive elements. We invest our own values in it; and words distort reality. Looking for it, thus, is like looking for a woman of the opposite sex.

American law professor Ronald Dworkin, a relativist, concluded: 'I see no point in trying to find some general argument that moral or political or legal or aesthetic or interpretative judgments are objective ... The whole issue of objectivity which so dominates contemporary theory in these areas is a kind of fake'. Hence the philosophical despondency, and what Iris Murdoch called 'the hygienic and dehydrated analysis of mental concepts', which in our postmodernist times are often articulated with new, original combinations of the well-known letters of the alphabet. Postmodernist 'complex ideas' necessitate, apparently, convoluted syntax, incoherent organisation, and pretentious jargon.

G. E. Moore, the founder of twentieth century Anglo-Saxon moral philosophy, described the 'thing good in itself' as something intrinsically good irrespective of its specific social or historical realities. Being a simple, unanalysable quality without any natural properties, it can, thus, neither be proved nor disproved; and looking for it is the blind man's search in a dark room for a black cat, which is not there. The English analytic philosopher A.J. Ayer, a fervent atheist, took the argument a step further and disarmed philosophy of any moral purpose. Philosophical theories, abstract as they are in search of conceptual truths, he said, do not make moral judgments. When it comes to that, they are as neutral as trigonometry. Detachment from the pains of life can always protect itself with good arguments. Hence Nietzsche's 'of all that is written, I love only what a man has written with his blood'.

Ludwig Wittgenstein, one of the most influential philosophers of the twentieth century and a man whose tormented personal life would have justified a passion which was not there, for the 'truth', had already argued that the business of philosophy is 'not a body of propositions, but to make propositions clear'. His position did not enhance his own respect for philosophy, this 'dishonest and pointless occupation', 'a kind of living death'. It did not help him, either, to face the Hitlerite reality of his time to which he remained stubbornly blind.

As it is, objective reality is only what we choose to see in it, and what we choose to see is affected by its bearing on our interests and wellbeing. We will, of course, readily agree that spring, which arrived yesterday at 13.00 hours, came five days and six hours earlier than it did when the records on spring arrivals began, or that Ashrita Furman, a New Yorker, covered a distance of 113.76 km balancing a milk bottle on his head in 18hr 46 min – a record according to my old, 1995, Guinness Book of Records. But when reality requires commitments that affect our personal interests, objectivity, just like a political prisoner 'trying to escape', jumps out of the sixth floor window.

Hence the warning, issued by the United Nations-sponsored International Panel on Climate Change that, if nothing changes, temperatures are bound to rise this century by up to 5.8°C with catastrophic consequences for many parts of the world, was for years contemptuously dismissed by the United States, by far the most air polluting country. The announcement by the UN-sponsored Panel was treated by Washington as seriously as that British housewife's statement to the effect that she always gives her husband sausages for breakfast. Unfortunately, the good and right, whose case is argued fervently in many languages though its champions cannot tell the truth in any of them, relates, not to itself, but to other considerations. It is practically never dissociated from expediency. Sophocles made the point early enough in his play *Philoctetes*.

In the story, Neoptolemus, Achilles' son, is asked by Odysseus to trick Philoctetes and steal from him his invisible bow and arrows. The bow and arrows had been given to Philoctetes by Heracles as a present for his goodness. Philoctetes, nevertheless, cruelly banished by his former comrades to the uninhabited island of Lemnos, and reduced by circumstances to a physically and emotionally pitiful figure, depended on his bow for his life.

Arguing the case to young Neoptolemus, Odysseus explains that the dishonourable act had to be committed as the Greeks would otherwise never capture Troy. 'We shall be justified in the end', he reassures the young man. Neoptolemus does not, however, seem convinced. 'There are things', he answers, 'that offend my conscience ... I'd rather lose by fair means than win by foul'. Odysseus, naturally, refuses to give up. 'Call me any names you like', he continues, 'the viler the better – I shan't mind. But remember', the Greeks have to win the war. Neoptolemus is, thus, persuaded to trick Philoctetes for the cause. 'I'll do it', he says at the end, 'and conscience can be hanged'. After he has done it, however, he feels nothing but revulsion for his 'base treachery against a fellow-creature', and returns the bow to Philoctetes while Odysseus draws his sword.

Although his heart was with Philoctetes, Sophocles did not have to declare himself in favour of the one side or the other. He was only a playwright. So, instead, he brought Heracles on the scene, and Heracles sorted things out to everybody's satisfaction. But the basic dilemma over the choice between country and humanity remained. As such, it encapsulates the modern conflict between the utilitarian, the modern Odysseus, and the Kantian, who would stand by Philoctetes, between the expedient and the ethical, the profitable and the moral, the useful and the right.

Utilitarianism, spreading from the Anglo-Saxon world, perceives the essence of good as 'the greatest happiness for the greatest numbers'. This understanding, noticed for its pragmatism, underpins liberal democracy but, as John Rawls argued, it should, with some very special exceptions to the rule, be considered as incompatible with all principles of Justice. The concept, introduced by Francis Stevenson, the father of utilitarianism, does not rub noses with the sunlight.

Medical research, for example, involving expendable humans for the benefit of mankind, torture of prisoners in Guantánamo for the extraction of information which can advance the American war aims, or the destruction of Hiroshima, cannot really be justified on the grounds that action of this kind brings happiness to the greatest numbers. Developed further by Jeremy Bentham, whom Charles Dickens and others considered inhumanly rational, and John Stuart Mill, utilitarianism set as its aim the pursuit of pleasure, which bourgeois G.E. Moore identified with the pleasures of human intercourse and the enjoyment of beautiful objects. This can end up as unadulterated eudaemonism.

Good as such has, therefore, no inherent value, for the rightness and the goodness of any action is made dependent solely on the benefits and the pleasure the group or the individual derives from them. Thrasymachus and Callicles, the Sophists, had already made the point when they extolled the virtues of a man who uses his intelligence to dominate, and uses his domination to satisfy his desires. They were dismissed by Socrates and Plato on the grounds that good and bad cannot be synonymous with pleasant and painful. Good could not simply be what men desire. Hobbes reiterated the Sophists' point by stating that good is what is good for one's own self. Man, seeking 'power after power that ceaseth only in death', is, thus, in a state of war with his fellow human beings – 'war of every man against every man'.

But pleasure as such offers no direction. In fact, Nietzsche dismissed it altogether, for 'man', he said, 'does not seek pleasure'. Rather puzzlingly, he added: 'only the Englishman does that'. Pursued for its titillations or one's self-interest attached both to itself and anything else equally profitable, pleasure-seekers, high on seediness or not, can use it to justify anything, from football hooliganism to racism, from hunting to genocide, from rape to 'humanitarian' bombing.

This attitude, reflected also in the way the individual acts, is content to sanction the means, whatever they are, to ends determined as good, not by morality, but power. As the eighteenth century American statesman Benjamin Franklin put it bluntly, virtues are a means to an end, the end being for him, as Scottish moral philosopher Alasdair MacIntyre pointedly commented, 'success, prosperity in Philadelphia and ultimately in heaven'. In the pursuit of expediency, a forest can, thus, disappear to make room for a golf course which will create new employment opportunities, a community can be split down the middle to allow for a new motorway which can save time, or arms can be exported to countries which have no respect for human rights if that helps 'our' manufacturers to grow and thrive. BAE, the British arms manufacturer, is a shining example of the latter. The goal is effectiveness and success, as highlighted in Erving Goffman's sociology, with success being whatever passes as success.

In its ugly form, utilitarianism is a denial of human feelings, the stifling of all values, the factory rule, as Nietzsche put it, which breeds hatred against culture. As 'Government House' utilitarianism, it is the renunciation of freedom in the interests of a calculative spirit directed ostensibly towards the common good. J.J.C. Smart, the Scottish-Australian philosopher, taking utilitarianism to the extreme, sent morality to the chthonian world. His view was that if our moral judgments conflict with the principle of utility so much the worse for them. 'The bishop farted loudly in St Paul's cathedral', Martial, the epigrammatist, said in a translation adapted to suit modern times; and 'the congregation lost some of its gravity'.

Utilitarianism does not just leave the doors wide-open to abuse of power by whatever establishment, political, scientific, technological or economic. It endorses it in advance. Hence, the de-politicisation of morality, its convenient association with sexuality and its subsequent confinement to the bedroom of our existence. But conventionality, as Charlotte Brontë remarked, is not morality.

Interestingly enough, postmodernism, though it rejects utilitarianism, together with the other values of the Enlightenment, including the autonomous individual, endorses it indirectly. The endorsement is in its anything-is-as-good-as-anything-else doctrine which sanctions the concept of good as good-is-what-is-good-for-me, i.e., the gains and the pleasure pursued by the utilitarians. But between the two there is also an important difference. While utilitarianism claims to be an ethical philosophy, postmodernism refuses to discuss ethics, which, it claims, can be assessed only in the context of their local normative framework. Good as a concept independent of contingencies is, thus, denied. Judgments can only be subjective.

This is bound to be the case for a long time to come unless objectivity gets a good agent to represent it.

2. A View From Nowhere

Universalism in its old forms has, just like the steam-powered buses, gone. But, though its pursuit has an adversarial element, the search for some universally accepted ethical standards cannot be arrested. However narrow-minded they may be, evaluations cannot be negated. First of all, authenticity demands from all living beings continuous involvement in value judgments, a feature of the human race constitutive of the social self and the individual's personal and social identity. As the Canadian philosopher Charles Taylor stated, 'to know who you are is to be oriented in moral space, a space in which questions arise about what is good or bad, what is worth doing and what not, what has meaning and importance for you and what is trivial and secondary'. All this involves value judgments which we cannot deny unless we are willing to deny our own selves.

But value judgments, if not arbitrary, need a commonly accepted foundation that can be offered neither by an external authority nor by our desires. Looking for the determining agent, and in total opposition to the divine truth as embodied in Luther's doctrines but also to the teleological aims of utilitarianism, Immanuel Kant, the philosopher of the Enlightenment, looked, thus, uncompromisingly for a supreme moral principle, transcendent as in Plato's theory of Forms or in Augustine's interior illumination perceived as a gift from God. Good for him was something good in itself because of its nature rather than circumstances or particularities, and could be determined by nobody else but by a person's own conscience subordinate to, and oriented by, the universal moral law which pre-exists our experiences and overrides context. Kant believed that morally sovereign, and concerned rather than indifferent, committed rather than complacent, and involved rather than disengaged, the individual would free himself from the tutelage of all external authorities and uninhibitedly take his own right path.

His categorical imperative, universal and internally consistent, was in this sense objectively given, guiding us as to what we 'ought' to do. 'Act', he wrote, 'only on that maxim which you can at the same time will to be a universal law'. His 'ought', underpinned by the Stoic quest for 'good, not as a means to some further end, but as an end in itself', demanded that the individual obey the pregiven moral law. In doing so, a person was expected to do his 'duty' just for the sake of doing it and without a thought about consequences or results. His moral law recognised that every human being has 'inalienable' rights, owed to each 'by virtue of his humanity' which entitle everyone to be treated as an end in himself.

'Act', he wrote in *The Moral Law*, 'in such a way that you always treat humanity, whether in your own person or in the person of any other, never simply as a means, but always as an end'. This, which captured the essence of the teachings of Socrates and his philosophical heirs, demanded an inner transformation, inner commitments beyond an oppressive self-love, which, moving in narrowing circles, estranges us from our own deeper selves and others.

His philosophy did not offer practical 'eternal' terms of reference, and did not articulate the purpose of human activity or its aspirations and ends. It did not generate 'self-help' books, either, for those who cannot help themselves. It remained, thus, open to abuse by both authority, upon which it can itself become parasitic, and by the individual, who, free to interpret it at will, can do anything provided he does it conscientiously. This is, indeed, what Adolf Eichmann, Hitler's administrator of the 'final solution', claimed in his trial he was doing: obeying his own morality educated in the categorical imperative; or what, in our own time, the Taliban militia government in Afghanistan claimed they were doing when destroying the country's cultural heritage: obeying a religious imperative. By doing, as he said, the 'right thing' which helped to open the floodgates to the horrors of Iraq, Tony Blair, the British prime minister, did not do anything different. But, perhaps, no theory is good enough to guide us if the opaque side of our existence cannot be brought under control, if we ourselves only too readily put the truth through the test of its final endurance.

Aristotle would have endorsed the point Kant made but only partially. The Greeks did not believe, as Kant did, in moral virtue which rested on a single and autonomous moral principle 'in accordance with its own eternal and unalterable laws', which, given to us *a priori*, i.e. prior to, and apart from, our experiences, had to be obeyed. Kant's metaphysical conception of the agent, the 'noumenal' self, residing neither in yesterday nor tomorrow but in the timeless expanses of forever, certainly related to a cosmic and universal order. This meant that there were things which a man could never be allowed to do whatever the circumstances. For example, 'if a man', Aristotle, who articulated to perfection the traditional Greek understanding of moral order, held, 'takes more than his share ... this is part of a universal injustice'. But, on the other hand, morality, as Aristotle held, being a human affair rather than a dogma originating in heaven, could not be an abstraction beyond our experiences, given *a priori*, as Kant believed. The natural and universal coexisted with the conventional, particular and local; and morality, rooted in society, was defined by both certain eternal norms and also by the particular society's specific features and standards as shaped by Reason as Logos and the ideals of the polis. Good was doing 'the right thing in the right way and at the right time'.

Kant's humanism, the kingdom of Christianity without God, still exerts a profound influence on the thinking of the West. It is the departure point for all schools of thought, Marxist or liberal, which have an inbuilt dislike of utilitarianism. For liberal political theory and moral philosophy, Kantianism provided a common basis for the evaluation of the legitimacy of forms. In social terms it was identified with fairness, and in legal terms with neutrality and impartiality. But the basic disagreements as to what is right and good for all was anything but resolved; and Justice's flag still has the colours of the rainbow. The existentialists, who, heavily influenced by Kant, argued that we must never will what cannot consistently be willed by all other rational beings, did not make the picture any clearer. Sartre's argument that when choosing we act not merely for ourselves, but for all men, as representatives of mankind, just highlighted the anguish, what Kierkegaard called the 'dizziness of freedom', the arduous human experience in choosing a life path.

Though Kant's impelling decency is of the kind which any person will instinctively recognise and respect, his doctrine failed completely to demarcate 'objectively' the foundations of universal goodness. His critics were too many for comfort. For postmodernism in particular, Kant's universalism is as appetizing as a ball of boiled stones served for breakfast.

Hegel objected to the abstraction of Kant's thesis, as ethics and Reason are, he held, 'impure', in other words, contextualised, arising out of experiences and the realities of life. Kant's notion of 'duty' has, likewise, degenerated into a bureaucratic concept – the duty of the civil servant, the soldier, the professional. For Hegel, man acts autonomously by exercising his free choice – for Nietzsche it was his will. But he also objected to the universality Kant gave to his moral and ethical views. The substance of the latter, Hegel said, is drawn, instead, from the existing social structures, the civil society, its ethical institutions and the family. They are, therefore, anything but the same everywhere regardless of time and place. A shopkeeper in San Diego can hardly be expected to share the same values held by a shopkeeper in Baghdad. Marx, on the other hand, though a Hegelian, had been taken in his youth by Kant. But as the years progressed, he left his early idealism behind. Morality, he thought, is an authority which no longer exists, and Kantianism, focusing on the consciousness of the individual rather than on social formations, ends up as a counter-revolutionary ideology.

Marx himself never searched for the meaning of goodness. He never appealed to Justice in order to make his case for the working class. Such an appeal had no meaning for him because it could only be made to those who were denying people the Justice he would be asking. Many moral precepts are, of course, assumed as common to all social classes because all of them are constituted by humans. But at the same time each class has its own morality and understanding of the right and the good. The absence of a shared form of social order precluded, thus, transcendent definitions beyond class divisions. But Marx, once described as 'a shoemaker' on the assumption that all revolutionaries must have impeccable working class credentials, never defined working class morality. Even worse, he never highlighted the morality of a communist society.

Hence Eduard Bernstein, the pre-1914 leader of the revisionist Marxist wing which established the modern German Social Democratic Party, fell back on the classless categorical imperative of Kant, whilst Karl Kautsky, the chief social democrat theorist, opted for a crude utilitarianism. Later Marxists, such as the Austro-Marxists, took Kant as a point of departure, accepting Kantian morality with utilitarianism as the ultimate arbiter of all practices.

Good as the 'view from nowhere', which underpinned Kant's accident-prone views, could not withstand the pressures of our era. The decentredness of postmodern society in particular and the corresponding multiplicity of values cannot accept a concept expressing the unity of an intersubjectively formed common will. Helped by the traditional society's current breakdown, which has deprived traditional terms of reference of their social anchorage, and content to doze in the shade of complacency called personal convictions, the contemporary individualistic culture and its trendy vagueness cannot assess values except in terms of 'me'. The only context is the 'me', one's own situation, position, beliefs, feelings and presumptions about the world as the latter is viewed from the outer edges of concern about anything of value to humans. Kant's individual is there, but good cannot be objectively defined. Its definition is a private affair, as personal as our hiccups. Being inflexible, Kant's understanding of the right and good was therefore self-defeating. Seen charitably today, his doctrine might elicit only messages of sympathy, even an invitation for tea with cucumber sandwiches.

But neither John Rawls, the American philosopher, nor Jürgen

Habermas abandoned their model of universalism. The former anchored it in a fairness springing from an inbuilt moral grammar that underlies human behaviour. His concept of it, as developed in his contractarian theory which was based on the principles of Justice, was assumed to rest on a hypothetical contract. Habermas, a man too nice for our times, looked for a rational consensus reached within an open, inclusive, spontaneous and intrinsically pluralistic public sphere that would embrace a fair and impartial moral norm. New York University Professor Ronald Dworkin, Yale University Professor Bruce Ackerman and Harvard Univesity Professor Frank Michelman, on the other hand, did not look for compatibility with independently established principles, but for a form of expressive convergence conceived nevertheless by each one of them along different lines. Reflective judgment reached this way, according to Dworkin, needs to be guided by integrity, understood as self-congruency or authenticity. Richard Mervyn Hare, the English moral philosopher, for his part, argued that if we are to commit ourselves to universal moral principles then we have to commit ourselves necessarily to some form of utilitarianism.

Others placed the emphasis on other virtues. Friedrich Nietzsche looked forward to the 'superman', him who he said is the antithesis to 'modern' and 'good' men, including 'Christians and other nihilists', and he cherished nobility, courage and honesty, the aristocratic will to power. Power for him was not power over others, but over oneself. Thornstein Veblen based his understanding of living a good life on the values of work, utility and industry, and Ivan Illich on austerity, modesty and hard work. Max Weber, for whom social structures exist only as the 'actual or the possible social actions of individual persons', underlined responsibility, Theodor Adorno extolled leisure, happiness, and freedom from utility, and Aldous Huxley, who in his later years was won by the occult, celebrated spiritual transcendence. Max Scheler, influenced by Nietzsche, sought a new 'spiritual aristocracy', Georg Simmel favoured an aesthetic way of being and Murray Bookchin, in Socratic fashion, opted for a 'just and honourable life'. Leo Tolstoy, on the other hand, convinced that being explicit and articulate about principles is morally crippling, extolled the peasant ways of being.

The Romantics, followed by the existentialists, depoliticising the good life and taking it out of its social and political context, placed the emphasis on sincerity and authenticity, a person's ability to be true to himself. Jaspers, though he held that an individual needs to reach out to others in order to establish a common ground for individual existence, failed to transcend the personal. The connection between the fundamental condition of individual existence and the world, between the personal and the political was simply not there. Even Martin Buber and Gabriel Marcel's talk of intersubjectivity tended to cover a person's intimate and domestic life rather than his relation to bureaucracies or the corporate world. R.H. Tawney insisted on the dignity and a refinement of individuals, the freedom to become themselves, and D.H. Lawrence, likewise, praised the virtues of spontaneity; the self's purpose, he said, is 'to come into the fullness of its being'.

Nothing, as a result, can be translated into single words – usually in plenteous supply when we have little or nothing to say – which can be universally applauded. No vision, whatever its odour or colour, can ever expect to secure the endorsement of every group or every single individual on the planet. The search for the right and the good, for the imprecise, expressing, as George Seferis, the poet, might say, 'desires that played like big fish in seas suddenly shrinking', seems to resemble the search for the origins of green.

Yet something in the whole picture denies both logical and moral legitimacy to the current relativism, the new God we are happy to worship. The analytical mind may be understandably unable to define the right and the good, but the right and the good is out there, grounded, as Jürgen Habermas said, in the structure of our experiences, trusted to represent the universal core of our moral intuitions. Its recognition may rely on a negotiated consensus, which transcends the opposition between 'us' and 'them', and may be subject to multi-interpretability. But, like an El Greco painting, full of distortions, exaggerated effects and ecstatic forms, it expresses the reconciliation of the temporal with the eternal, the finite with the infinite, intellectual perceptions with unconscious drives. It is, as Aristotle said, the sum total of both the standards of a particular society and also of certain eternal norms. But yet, in a language without an alphabet which neither ages nor like the salmon dies after reproduction, it defines the truth in relation, not to the best-funded research, but only to itself.

The standards set by this negotiated consensus are in several instances totally unquestionable. We do not, for example, eat people, we do not take slaves any more, or we do not admit to it, and we do not kill a man's servants upon his master's death so that service can continue to be provided in the afterlife. Our action is guided in such instances by some objective criteria rooted, whatever the nature of society, in certain commonly accepted evaluative truths, in certain features of human life which are the common property of mankind and in certain beliefs in eternal moral laws. The same criteria fill us with an inner satisfaction when Julia Roberts, taking on the chemical industry single-handedly, or Steven Seagal, fighting gallantly against the oil industry, manage against all odds to win the day.

Though its universalised concept is dismissed as oppressive, human nature is not culturally determined. It is not, therefore, variable from one society to another – we are all part of the 'same old river', as Leo Tolstoy put it. The animalistic states of the human being – 'fight and flight' reactions and primary fears or emotions, as Charles Darwin showed in 1872 – are both innate and universal. So is, as Noam Chomsky said, the innate cognitive capacity of the mind which is guided by 'a mass of schematisms, innate governing principles', 'something biologically given' and 'unchangeable'. There is nothing culturally determined in the screams of the mutilated victims of air bombardments and the crying of orphaned babies, in joy and pain, sadness and anger, enjoyment and fright, in blushing, a raised eyebrow or smiling eyes.

'Certain features of human life', Alasdair MacIntyre argued, are 'necessarily or almost inevitably the same in all societies' as there are 'certain evaluative truths which cannot be escaped'. Searching for what is common is not like consulting maps of the unknown. One can, thus, safely assume that we all want a pollution-free environment and a world safe from nuclear annihilation, crime or epidemics. We all look forward to the elimination of pain, from headaches to famine or genocide, and to a guarantee that our existence will be respected regardless of ideological, religious, political or economic structures. We all have the same secrets, and nothing private in our expectations, or, as the eighteenth century English essayist and poet Samuel Johnson put it, 'we are all prompted by the same motives, all deceived by the same fallacies, all animated by hope, obstructed by danger, entangled by desire, and seduced by pleasure'.

Whatever philosophy thinks about the objective foundations of mankind's truths, honesty, love, courage, solidarity or self-denial do also provide us with a kind of transcendental deduction of norms for all places and times. Truth is, somehow, out there, and distrusting it, as Empedocles said in the age of innocence, is only the evil man's attempt to place it under his power.

True, attempting to demarcate concepts such as femininity or 'natural' forms of sexuality, easier to recognise than define, is as safe as walking into a minefield on a wet Monday morning. Human behaviour cannot be regulated. But the substance and the boundaries of the freedoms of the individual are anything but unregulated. We are not, and we accept it, free to murder, steal or rape, discriminate, at least in public, against ethnic minorities, sell cocaine in café bars or drive above the speed limit. We cannot even have a good riot before or after an England football game. Whether we would conform with these restrictions if we were to find the ring of invisibility, as Gyges, the Lydian shepherd, did, is an entirely different matter – Gyges, taking advantage of his invisibility, seduced his Queen and, with her help, murdered his King and then seized the throne.

In any case, we cannot do what we might otherwise be tempted to do if we did not have to observe the law and take into account issues of public health and safety, the accepted morality of the time or public standards ranging from town planning regulations to pub closing times. Our highly regulated world has set standards, fenced its functions and drawn borders to our activities which we cannot cross without punishment or at least embarrassment. The same world often does not even seek the agreement of all parties to a problem. Assuming that what they do is objectively right, the anti-drug law-enforcement agencies do not seek the blessing of their activities by the drug barons.

The limits of what is socially acceptable does expand or contract. Whatever the case, these limits rest, however, on a commonly accepted sense of an objectively defined common good. The sole genuine limitation that democracy can bear, Cornelius Castoriades, the Greek philosopher, said is self-limitation; and this is what we do – we limit ourselves in pursuit of the common good. Still our relativist, individualistic culture is only too ready to deny this common good; for if it did not, it would have to reappraise its ordinary, impersonal indifference, the new ideology for the masses, the soporific tune that sustains our hibernating existence. If truth, as something objectively given, cannot be found, this is not because we banished her to the New Hebrides of our consciousness for unreliability. It may well be because she herself, disgusted at our doubts, left us without a forwarding address.

The universal challenges are there requiring universal answers which rest on some sort of universal values. The latter, living monuments to an unageing discernment, the bedrock of our timeless, sempiternal virtue, cannot be dismissed even in an age as unyielding as ours if we are to survive as real rather than virtual human beings. The search for them has, indeed, not been abandoned even if their essence is sometimes disagreeable. Ideology, which Hannah Arendt, reflecting upon the Nazi and Stalinist horrors, identified with totalitarianism, if it stands for the supreme truth by which everything is judged and to which everything else is subordinated, is anything but dead. It is the hidden form of power behind all disagreeable -isms, from evangelism and islamism to racism and nationalism. Liberal imperialism, which enables the US, the 'sun', to control 'the planets, the moons and the asteroids', i.e. the rest of the world, is among its most virulent forms.

Insomniac memories, and dreams burdened, as poet Pablo Neruda would say, 'with moral remains', do make sure that the search for a world that makes sense is not abandoned. It has to be so, if the dream, embodying like marriage our hopes rather than experiences, is to remain awake.

3. Elusive But Extant

In the past, before sociology became the interpreter of our realities, men tended to blame fate for their misfortunes. But, rather disobligingly, Democritus, the fifth century BC philosopher, argued that 'men create the image of fate to excuse their own lack of thought'. Equally uncharitably, a century or so later Menander, the comic dramatist, added: 'you blame fate but the fault lies in your own character'. Reality was the challenge for the Greeks rather than fate; and men determined their destiny by the choices they made, achieved it rather than succumbed to it. As Aeschylus explained, fate confronts man with a choice, but the choosing is eventually his. Agamemnon, the Commander-in-Chief of the Greek campaign against Troy, 'put on, of his own free will, the harness of necessity'. But, as it happened, he made the wrong choice and earned his fate, for he was, as his wife, Clytaemnestra, put it, like 'a net, all holes'.

Choices do not come, however, in unlimited quantities. On the one hand, nobody forces us to be racists, Catholics or art-collectors, fathers, accountants or French speakers. No natural force has determined, either, that we rely for our diet on fish and chips or prawns cooked in dolphin's milk. But, on the other, we depend for our survival on adapting to the conditions in which we live, and in doing so we have no choices. Rather than hunt for our food, we tend to look for a job, rather than horses we use cars, and rather than pay with garlic, onions or milk we use credit cards to buy all the things we need. Mankind cannot transcend the context within which it functions, including the aspects of the context responsible for the structure and the force of its will. Disempowerment is inherent in this condition, for choices, decisions and actions are determined by the whole and its system of dependencies.

The world makes sure we do not escape. Imperceptibly programmed the moment we are born, we cannot run away from our realities. Our culture and all its unconscious assumptions and paralogisms, our socio-economic situation and its underlying structures, our nationality, history, race, language or religion make sure of it. A person's hopes and expectations, his or her values and sense of moral responsibility, the purpose and the goals in life are all conditioned by our environment – family, the given power relationships, the economic climate, social perceptions, the advances in technology, the history of every single issue of importance. We are determined by necessities, natural, economic, psychological, and by fears – of each other, of failure, of emotions, of exclusion, or of loneliness, unemployment and crime. The need for security has led to the repression of our instinctual drives, restricted our freedom and enforced moral compromises. A non-repressive civilisation, Freud has said, is an impossibility – hence some wish they could go back to the womb.

The freedom to choose is further denied by the zenithal distortion of our priorities, when our personal desires fail to resist the lure of the market. Man, turned by capitalism into a means to an end, an end which, as Alberto Moravia, the Italian novelist, said, is 'no man's business', is marginalised by his own needs, which are the system's needs. Illusion replaces reality, happiness is sought in the insubstantial world of image, and personal consciousness, the signifier of the individual's autonomous existence, ends up not being personal at all. Alienated from its inner core, de-individualised, socialised, it becomes as personal as a Euro-coin and as inimitable as a car. It is no longer 'us' but the world out there whose sense of the essential slides into the consciousness of the individual like an eel into a rock, and then, reappropriated, is owned like our liver.

Capitalism has always proclaimed the autonomy of the individual which, as it happens, legitimises the existing power structure. Individuals, it proclaims, have free choice, consumer choice, the spiritual element of the corybantic frenzy leading to multiple orgasm in the high street. The right to choose, a right won in battlefields by previous generations, is obviously honoured in the supermarket where, as Harriet Griffey demonstrated in *The Paradox of Choice*, we are absolutely free to buy any of 275 different varieties of cereal, 360 types of shampoo, 120 different pasta sauces or 175 types of tea bags. Discerning individuals, committed to tasteful choices and perpetual instant gratification, we remain, thus, convinced that our actions reflect our own free will, which, orgulously displayed in the day's living room, underpins our unique existence.

Yet, in spite of all the spurious liberties, the plethora of choices and also the presumed uniqueness of each individual's lifestyle, the only virtue of free will that is being appreciated lays in our submission to the socially maintained 'system of sentiments'. Capitalism, in any case, is doing more than at any other point in its history to destroy personal autonomy and individuality. The choices we do actually have are only those that the powerful vested interests, and the structures within which they operate, allow us to have. Subliminally, they convince us that what we really want is exactly what they want us to want. They formulate our needs, shape our desires, mould our fantasies making everyone look like everyone else: one face in many forms.

As a result, personal autonomy atrophies, becomes its shadow, the face of emptiness in lipstick, the knavish image of an idea. Free will, which never disappears, thus, spends its life in a context that represses it, personal autonomy survives but in conditions that negate it, and individuality is sustained but in circumstances that deny it. Like Gregor Samsa in Kafka's short story *The Metamorphosis*, who awoke one morning to find himself metamorphosed into a gigantic insect, the freedom which is granted to us the moment we are born can, without our knowing, turn from an oak tree into a geranium on top of the dishwasher.

Escaping from our world, its structures and assumptions, its expectations, hopes, fears and frustrations, the spirit of routine, salaried or otherwise, or as D.H. Lawrence said, 'the settled habits of a vast living incomprehensibility', is a near-impossibility. Freedom as an abstract notion bears little resemblance to its realities.

The thesis supporting the dissolution of the self, the destruction of the individuals' personal identity, the loss of authenticity and, in the last analysis, the absence of freedom has considerable force behind it. The enduring legacy of the last two centuries has made sure that human action is interpreted within institutional and cultural structures – invisible and yet determining, 'present everywhere and visible nowhere' as novelist Gustave Flaubert said when talking about an author who in his book must be just like God. The autonomy of the subject has, indeed, been denied by nearly all schools of thought. Hobbes and Hume, Rousseau, Marx, Freud and Durkheim, Robert Owen, Nietzsche, Adorno and de Saussure, William James, Althusser, Poulantzas, Lacan, Irigaray, Foucault and Derrida – they have all proclaimed that the freedom of the individual is to varying degrees limited, or fully denied, by civilisation and its social, economic, cultural, or political structures, its ideology and language, 'reality' or its symbolic order, the 'will to power', the 'iron necessity', or in our days by technology believed by both financial markets and policy-makers to be the force that determines our lives. Georg Lukács emphasised the process of homogenisation that the heterogeneity of everyday life is subjected to, and Jürgen Habermas denounced the instrumental rationalisation that has eroded the emancipatory communicative potential of everyday life.

Power is in the hands of man's creations, those of the monster in Mary Shelley's Frankenstein; or, for the New Agers, in the hands of fate decoded by numerologists, crystal ball and Tarot card readers, psychics, clairvoyants, channelers, astrologers and others. Man, Jean-Jacques Rousseau said, is born free, but he is everywhere in chains.

The autonomy of the individual, denied by our circumstances, cannot, however, be negated. Even if they live and breed in battery conditions, it is humans who turn the wheels of history. The wheels do not turn by themselves. Herbert Marcuse acknowledged the individuals' standardised reaction pattern established by the hierarchy of power and functions and by its repressive technical, intellectual and cultural apparatus. But, as he emphasised, whatever the circumstances, personality does not disappear. It continues to flower, albeit in a way that fits and sustains the socially desired pattern of behaviour and thought, thereby cancelling individuality itself. Language, both verbal and nonverbal, is, likewise, manipulative, but its manipulation operates within the cultural perimeters we all recognise, and is encoded in a way we can all decipher. When Tony Blair talked about the 'Third Way', which at least at the beginning some thought was a religious cult, a sexual position or a plan to widen the M25, we all knew what he meant – nothing. Language could not wipe out the fingerprints nothingness had left on his pronouncement. The impact of manipulative organisational or personal behaviour is, thus, albeit not significantly, reduced by shared understandings, assumptions, experiences, beliefs and expectations.

Though often frustrated, the thrust to live a life in tune with one's inner truths is always there. Humans cannot be reduced to systems, which, as Pericles said, cannot even be trusted. What we trust, he told the Athenian Assembly, is, instead, 'the spirit of our citizens'.

This 'spirit' has not dissolved into thin air. The passionate, the romantic, the mystical, the chimerical, the wild side of our being, though often lethargic, is still with us. *L' amour de l'exactitude* cannot, as Delacroix, the French Romantic painter, said, be mistaken for the truth – the intellect may well demand accuracy, but the soul still craves meaning. After all, as Aristotle explained, the soul is not only one thing: a part of it is rational and another part irrational. No matter how much the information revolution may achieve, we will still love and hate, get happy or depressed, feel proud or ashamed, fancy, desire, dream, imagine or fear, and we still need intimacy, a few friends, children to enliven our lives and green fields in which our eyes, ears and mind can have a rest. The message our washing machine can send to our mobile telephone to inform us that the washing cycle has been completed is not going to change our very human nature.

Moreover, we loathe being compelled or coerced. We need to be, or at least to feel we are, free from external pressures, able to determine, and be, ourselves, to choose our course of action and satisfy our needs in a variety of ways. After all, perversity, as John Updike, the American novelist, remarked, is the soul's very life. Freedom, although its manual has gone missing, is, indeed, a condition of survival, the fundamental element that gives meaning and purpose to life, the highest prize a person can win in the struggle to assert his or her own self in a hostile environment. Freedom is also what ensures the supremacy of the animated world over its inanimate creations – dogmas, systems and machines, structures, commodities and needs.

The existentialist philosophers took the humanistic argument to its logical conclusion. Like the Romantics for whom the individual was the 'hero' of his own life, Karl Jaspers, in a way reminiscent of Protagoras' 'man is the measure of all things', said that 'man is everything'. This 'everything' is nevertheless, as Sartre, Camus, Marcel, Tillich, Jaspers and Heidegger held, dehumanised by technology and institutions which turned human beings into slaves of their functions. The human being, Heidegger said, is 'forlorn' and 'abandoned'.

In spite of the 'radical absurdity' or the meaninglessness of the world, man can, however, ultimately make his own choices. Consciousness, the awareness, or rather the process, which accesses, interprets, and gives meaning to reality, is as a concept notoriously elusive. For William James, a representative of American philosophical pragmatism, it does not even exist. Material reality and consciousness are certainly not identical. But at the same time they are not ontologically opposed, external to each other. Being parts of the whole, engaged in a causal interaction, they are both integral parts of a whole process which transforms both consciousness and reality itself. Life, in other words, has an irreducible subjective side which leaves open as many options as both human unpredictability and the search for freedom allow for. It is not a factory producing standardised items according to specifications.

To augment an independent and authentic personal identity, existentialism expanded the Kantian concept to include a critical reflection on all culturally determined values and goals. Humanity, Heidegger argued, was achieved by our ability to question being, or 'being there', 'there' being represented by the actual world. He, thus, placed his emphasis on the individuals' ability to make decisions, the responsibility they are prepared to assume for themselves. So did Albert Camus, the French existentialist philosopher and novelist who was killed in a car crash in 1960. Life, he said, depends solely on us rather than circumstances. Still, for Camus, the symbol of mankind is Sisyphus, the hero who kept rolling a boulder to the top of a hill only to see it rolling back.

For his part, Jean-Paul Sartre insisted that we are not prisoners of some predetermined natural order like stones. 'Existence precedes essence'; man *becomes* rather than is. Human beings, Sartre explained, are not only what they conceive themselves to be, but also what they will themselves to be after the thrust towards existence. For Sartre, what is not possible is not to choose, for a man who makes no decisions has no existence. Man is not condemned to die in debt for all the things promised to himself and never given. If he is, Camus said, he might as well commit suicide. The freedom the existentialists proclaim is closely linked, albeit for some of them, with moral responsibility – we do not choose merely for ourselves, but, as representatives of mankind, for all men; and the meaning of this act, Sartre said, 'is integrated as a secondary structure in global structures and finally in the totality which I am'.

On the same path, the personal development movement seeks the self-realisation of the individual through the unhindered development of his or her potentials. 'Human existence and freedom', Erich Fromm stated emphatically, 'are from the beginning inseparable'. But freedom, which must be reconquered at every moment and through every act, cannot be private and asocial. It has to be achieved, Fromm insisted, in unity with people and in rational social action. Incidentally, self-realisation, placing man, rather than God, at the centre of the universe, incurred Pope John Paul's displeasure. Salvation, his spokesman said, would come only through Christ, and not through our own works.

Although its philosophical origins are different, evolutionary psychology, i.e. Darwinism with a human face, which grew in opposition to a crude sociobiological Darwinism that has been used to justify aggression, rejected the notion that human nature is profoundly malleable. Benevolent, albeit profoundly disturbed, we still have a good chance of making it. After all, the world is not unchangeable like the calendar, and natural selection has not eliminated trust, generosity, unselfishness, altruism or cooperation on which complex relationships for the common good can be built. Here, again, the future can be in the hands of humans rather than God, events or systems.

This being the case, we can all drive off cheerfully to the nearby summer theatre to enjoy, as Canadian writer Margaret Atwood suggested, a few relaxing hours of treachery, sadism, adultery and murder.

4. Battle For Your Own Sake

The freedom of the individual to be whom he chooses, his ability to make choices which, as Karl Jaspers put it, is what existence is about, man's fundamental capacity to be 'nothing else but what he makes of himself', as Jean-Paul Sartre said time and again, is the core of the existentialist position. For the existentialists, nothing is predetermined and nothing is a prior condition of man's existence. A man's worth is what man himself puts into his existence. This does not necessarily mean that a member of Burundi's Tutsi tribe is as likely as a white European to become a Pasteur, born to invent the inoculation against anthrax. But either of them can choose not to sell his integrity in return for material benefits, or, as Thales put it with such superb simplicity, refrain from doing the things he would blame others for doing. The existentialist position is, in this sense, the Stoic declaration of faith in the strength, the inborn ability of man to maintain his humanity intact without calculation or ulterior motives, untouched by consequences and irrespective of results.

Dignified though it is, existentialism fails to connect choice with its social, political or economic realities, as it fails to give the concept of authenticity an ethical dimension. Its moral judgments rest on the choices made by the individual in accordance with his or her personal feelings, morally upgraded through, perhaps, an intensive course in corporative ethical announcements. Postmodernism, on the other hand, would argue that the notion of innate humanist ideas presupposes an intolerable essentialism to which we cannot subscribe. Still the notion of an ethical disposition cannot really be challenged even when moral and ethical claims conflict with each other. Cultural differences cannot justify the moral flexibility that is so often associated with Justice; and the preservation of life and what life values cannot, and do not, depend on the context in which they are debated.

'Context' matters but so does personal choice. Nothing carries greater authority, Sartre insisted, than a person's own choices about the right and the good. Under the same set of circumstances, one, guided by a good sense of the right and the good, can be on the road to sainthood, and another, misguided, on the road to crime. Or, to use historian of ideas Isaiah Berlin's example, if someone saved you from drowning, you do not tell him he could not avoid doing this because he was so made by his context. You just thank him for risking his life to save you. His selfless act has nothing to do with his being a traditionalist or a postmodernist, educated or not, Greek or Korean, black or white. Another person with the same qualities could equally well pretend he had not seen a thing. What is important here is what one is, not what one consumes or does. Only the vulgar, Hannah Arendt insisted, will condescend to derive pride from what he is doing.

But the criteria on the strength of which 'right' and 'wrong' can be 'objectively' determined have not taken by storm the Bastille of our reservations. Even simple and straightforward moral issues, like not killing another human being, lose all meaning in a different context such as that provided by the Iraq war.

Kant connected the personal choice to pure Reason as interpreted by the individual, and David Hume, believing that there are no objective properties on the strength of which one can define virtuousness, transferred the field where moral judgments are made from Reason to sentiment. Others, incuding Hobbes, connected it to intuition. G.E. Moore subsequently developed the theory of moral intuition, which, he held, could guide us to the heart of goodness without the backing of any valid rational justification regarding objective and impersonal moral standards. But as philosopher Philippa Foot put it, talking about intuitions which can 'stand the test of time' or those which reflect the views of 'more highly developed peoples' is 'simply a cheat'. The notion 'a man's got to do what a man's got to do' becomes, thus, for intuitionism only or primarily an 'I approve of it', as meaningless for strict rationalists as the appeal to common sense.

Jean-Jacques Rousseau adopted a different approach. If we consult our conscience, he held, we may go astray intellectually, but not morally. His simple and powerful assumption was that human nature, thought distorted by the corruption of existing social and political institutions, is fundamentally good. Moved by self-love, all natural man wanted, he said, was 'food, a woman and sleep'; and all he feared was 'pain and hunger'. Conscience has been for others, too, the secular society's God, whom we either honour or, if we cannot, we might as well displace with a last, postchristian, divine God to be born. But 'the voice of conscience' as the sacred and absolute authority, though loud enough for the head to hear, has been dismissed by many other thinkers, from Hume to Maslow.

The assumption that man is good by nature can be easily questioned after all the centuries have witnessed. But as many still believe, the commitment to do the 'right thing' can be made to nobody but one's own better self, to what Paul Tillich, the existential theologian, called one's own 'essential nature'. The strength of his thesis is drawn from the basic nature of the human being, which, despite its failures, can be assumed to be constructive and trustworthy.

The Greeks did not exactly make this assumption. Instead, rather in the 'essential nature' of the humans, they placed their faith in man's intelligence, for an intelligent man would never misidentify the object of his desires and do the morally wrong thing. Morality rested on Reason, the Greeks' Logos. Yet, judging by the 'I bomb therefore I am' American response to whatever challenges American authority, one can easily conclude that intelligence must have disappeared from earth – and for a good long time.

Unfortunately, as Aristotle held, the dark side of human nature, hidden like the moon's, is always there, for it is the nature of the many to be ruled by fear rather than shame. Many, he held, refrain from evil not because of the disgrace but because of the punishments. It can, as a result, be assumed that life is a dialectical interaction between the positive and the negative, and, rather than conform with a preordained pattern of goodness, it is a challenge daily facing each one of us.

Goodness, as the Greeks believed, had, therefore, to be cultivated, taught to the young, improved by the use of a man's intelligence, and studiously practised in everyday life. Habits were considered to be the best guarantee of goodness, and habits develop socially within a given culture. As Democritus put it, 'more men are good by practice than by nature' – Ludwig Wittgenstein thought, likewise, that the criterion of right action is embodied in the rules of the socially established practice. And the best way to cultivate the intellectual virtues of wisdom, intelligence, and prudence was through education. The objective, as Aristotle said, was to build a just and honourable character, which would reflect both the inner nature of goodness and man's drive to perfection. To this end, for Plato, some help from a philosophical midwife would be quite handy.

The man of just and honourable character whom the Greeks had in mind was not, however, the enlightened intellectual sought by a number of Western thinkers. The people to reform the world were not Wilhelm von Humboldt's 'aristocracy of talent and character', Mannheim's 'intellectuals' or Huxley's 'élite' which could guide a self-governing and balanced community. They were not Matthew Arnold's individuals, either, those in each class who are led 'by a general humane spirit, by the love of human perfection', and their active best self, nor William Morris' 'minority culture', the one which guards the standards, sets the future trends, and articulates humankind's long term aspirations. These people, of relatively small numbers, can, indeed, influence the choices of the majority, alter the course of events, even act as a catalyst in social and cultural terms. In communion with the uncreated, they ignite the brainstorms which can transform the landscape of our thinking. But granting them the claimed leading role has dangerously illiberal implications. The answer, as the Greeks believed, can only be a community of leaders within the context of the city.

The individual had to be open to the world, and prepared to

interact with the community. This is only natural as human practice is directed to something other than one's own self and engages the individual in a relationship with the world. As Abraham Maslow, one of the prime movers of humanistic psychology, put it, 'there is no such a thing as blushing without something to blush about'. Blushing always means 'blushing in context'. The context is the world, which, when we are awake, is, as Heraclitus pointed out, one and common to us all – one turns to one's own world only when asleep. This world is guaranteed by the presence of others and our relationship with them in the public realm.

The individual's goal in such a context is to 'share words and deeds' as Thucydides, the historian, put it, act together with other humans to win and maintain the power which belongs to humans rather than constellations of interests and their non-human creations. If this power, Arendt maintained, is 'not actualised, it passes away, and the greatest material riches cannot compensate for this loss'. Inaction is, therefore, not an option.

Action is necessary regardless of personal consequences or desired results. When, for example, in the old days I used to join the 'ban the bomb' marches, organised by the CND, I had no illusions that these marches could persuade the leaders of the nuclear Powers to end the nuclear arms race and eliminate the means of mass destruction. Yet, unwilling to surrender my right to live, I kept attending them so that on the morning of the day I heard on the radio that missiles had been launched I could tell myself that I had done all I could to avert the move from the last war to the last war. I could then kiss the earth between my hands and say goodbye in peace with myself.

My own obstinate refusal to live with the madness of our world is idiosyncratic up to a point – it reflects this inherent rebelliousness, a survivor, to be shot down on sight by any card-carrying feminist, of this almost extinct notion, the quaint sense of discernment according to which 'a man's got to do what a man's got to do' – light, if he has to, his cigarette from the shells whizzing past his nose. But it certainly has more to it than my simple, and for better or worse improving, imperfections can contribute. It was choice, the choice which, whatever the circumstances, cannot be taken away from any human being, what defines one's essence, and gives selfhood a meaning beyond what a Madonna concert, a Higher Income Plus ISA or a Tikka Masala can provide.

All I could, and still can, unfortunately, do as a single individual is effectively nothing – I do not possess a secret book to make a secret sign and wait, like Faust, for the spirit to appear in the flame to fulfil my wishes. But, on the other hand, I cannot just sit and enjoy, in contented repose, the garden of my interior culture regardless of what happens to humans, the planet, the poor, democracy, or our own selves even if and when people cast doubt on the meaning of the words 'human', 'planet', 'poor', 'democracy' or 'self'.

Despite its brilliantined wording, 'indifference', which French cultural theorist Jean Baudrillard suggested is the masses' 'original strategy', their effective method of self-defence, is nothing more than a sole commitment to apathy, to doing nothing about anything, and doing it very well. Hiding behind words such as relativism, the subterfuge of our evasions, or realism, the face of cowardice in lipstick, only sustains this supercilious and scornful attitude of nubile detachment, which, at least as long as the salt of youth is still in me, will never be my 'strategy'. This can only be the 'strategy' of the dead in the floating island of obmutescence. Personal autonomy occurs not by avoiding evil, but by directly confronting it even if evil itself is still waiting for philosophy to give it an 'objective' definition.

We do, of course, feel disheartened by the increasing powerlessness, the galloping marginalisation, the growing parochialism of the individual in the global village, the 'suffocating spaciousness' of the new enforced solitude. As disheartening is the realisation that our voice is as ear-piercing as the moonlight. The result is this terrifying lack of collective self-consciousness towards the world, the disengagement of the individual from it, and the search for fulfilment in escapism, religious or otherwise. Despite all odds nothing should, however, be allowed to interfere with our judgment and undo our humanity. Whatever the results, nothing but action within the world can enable a person to call himself legitimately alive. 'We can't just look on', Günter Grass, the German novelist, cried almost in despair. 'Even if we can't stop anything we must say what we think'.

Battles need to be fought even if the prospect of winning them is virtually non-existent, even if the gypsy girl will never dance for you. They just have to be fought. These are the battles between Reason and unreason, good and evil, right and wrong, the better and the worse part of ourselves. 'You fight in the wild wastes and know you'll never win', Nicos Kazantzakis defiantly declared, 'but still battle for your own sake'.

It was in the same spirit that Socrates had as defiantly stated before him: 'I would rather die having spoken after my manner than speak in your manner and live'. It is this courage that is needed if hope is not to disappear in a world totally corrupted by numerical certitudes and technological delusions, the merciless power of money; and, perhaps self-respect and dignity on which independent existence rests can only be won in striding rather than tiptoeing in life, in being strong, as T.S. Eliot said, 'beyond hope and despair', in freedom to choose, not your mobile's personalised ring tone, but who you are. In this 'lies man's true freedom', Bertrand Russell stressed. In such circumstances, action in futility, rather than disgraceful, is more profound, honourable and dignified.

This is, indeed, the ultimate test on which a person's character is judged, the basis on which personal achievement can be built, and the fundamental requirement of freedom: the freedom to choose to be yourself, even if you cannot be the hero of your own life, even if your personal history will not even name a small road after you, the person who has built its cities of joy and pain. Of importance is only the person's attributes, the pursuit of quality before quantity, nobility before achievement, and honour before opulence. These were the qualities Electra possessed, and her sister, Chrysothemis, did not, only to be demolished by Electra's 'I admire your caution but I despise your spirit'.

Electra's response, short, pungent, and verdant, wholly unforgettable, reflects of course the ethos of a bygone era, the heroic. It epitomises a person's inner strength, his or her essence, undiluted by the claims of personality. I am aware, of course, that today her fortitude and courage in defence of her truth would only too easily be crushed by the scorn of the cynics' glance.

'Good old Watson', I can almost hear Sherlock Holmes say, 'you are the only fixed point in a changing world'. In moments without a home address, I do feel, indeed, like Watson, Horace Walpole's inspired idiot, a dotty missionary preaching vegetarianism to tigers. It could hardly be otherwise at a time when people seem to be interested, not in the quintessence of truth, but in its white, tender skin, cream-lotioned and perfumed, and when many would argue that we need commitment as much as a fly needs the spider's web. It is then that the optimism of the heart is forced, as Gramsci was obliged to admit, to give way to the pessimism of the intellect, and doing the right thing looks like a madman's battle against the grotesque, watched by the latter with detached curiosity, even a mild amusement disorientedly offered free of charge. Going against the grain is certainly not going to bring years of grace with three Saturdays a week.

Individuals, determined to extend their horizons far beyond the impaired vision of the system, will, as they have always done, battle and often fail. The desirable is never within reach. But the battle has to be fought: for our sake, the sake of our descendents, the earth and all it supports, our soul. 'Our war', as Primo Levi, the Italian poet, urged the aged partisans, 'is never over'.

If God knew how impossible the human condition is, he would have felt the same.

Part II: Looking Inwards

1. From Postmodern to Postmortem

Realities are hard to change and hence, rather than engage in the unending struggle to improve what is at least seemingly beyond improvement, many simply choose to bypass it. As postmodernism has decreed, reality is only what you choose to see in it, and 'objective truth', though inimitable, is still as private as our dreams. Materialism, consumerism and hedonism, the new holy trinity that underpins our nihilism, made certain of it. With the path to the privatisation of truth eased, life on earth was, thus, freed from the patronage of its traditional godfathers, including God, His lieutenants and His authorised interpreters. Mecca, Rome or Jerusalem are no longer. Gone, too, were the rituals. Good Friday is 'a normal trading day', a Manchester United F.C. spokesman said arguing against the Church which had expressed its displeasure at the timing of a football match.

The spiritual vacuum, which only a high-spirited, ethical society could fill, became, thus, inevitable. In the absence of such a society, the mystics stepped in. 'Truths' may no longer be out there, in the world, but they exist, they claimed, in the land beyond the grasp of our senses, accessible to the 'eyes of the soul' and sold with a life-long guarantee not to disturb the enjoyment of our opulence. Religious fundamentalism staged a comeback even in the West. But its doctrines never managed to match the mass appeal of an amorphous spirituality, the New Age's, that turned out to be as fashionable as Kate Moss' clothing line.

The God of the New Age, an 'It' without a name, a face, a gender, racial characteristics or a family, without a history or authorised biographers, appearing in shapeless forms, all available in the world's spiritual supermarket for the benefit of the discerning individual, took the place of the old one. The Age of Aquarius, 'an age of splendour and of light' that places the emphasis on 'humanity, kindness, truth, spirituality and enlightenment' instead of 'possessions, money and other people', had dawned. Spiritual postmodernism had been born.

Just like philosophical postmodernism, the New Age, quasi-religious, turned against the Enlightenment and the power of Reason, and rejected all that modernist madness represents. But it also spurned all worldly affairs. Its real world, so improbable that it could almost exist, is beyond what the eyes can see, out of the range of our experiences, unaffected by our exertions. 'Invisible, unmediated, unmitigated and faster than light', it can neither be perceived by the senses nor explained in terms of causes in the immediate space-time vicinity. In the windowless nights of its eternity, objective forms, truth, can be seen only by 'the eyes of the soul'. Carl Jung, a spiritual man, able to smell the presence and hear the coughing of souls, saw, he said, the light beyond our illusory world. Having done so, he thought himself absolved of the obligation to oppose the Nazi nightmare. The eternal light was on but the dark of the small infinities and the very ordinary solicitudes remained.

Intoxicated by the mystical music broadcast live from the stars, Alice Bailey, the Manchester-born architect of the 'Age of Aquarius', described reality as 'energy itself and nothing else' – spirit and energy are synonymous terms, interchangeable. All the rest, the reality we all understand as such, are 'only the fogs and miasmas of the planes of illusion'. Truth and reality, unaware of their own nonexistence on the visible part of the world, cadaverous as sanctimoniousness in grief, are exiled to the vaporous infinity of the beyond. Relegated to the domain of the postmodernist personal 'truth', indefinable, unverifiable and inaccessible to all but the mystic, they become, if I may borrow a line from W.B. Yeats, a mystic himself, 'a something incompatible with life'.

The new focus was exclusively on the 'soul', which the English language, Gurdjieff, the mystic, said, pronounces and even writes almost like the 'sole'. Truth is reachable only through its eyes, i.e. an intuition operating at the edge of silence and the frontier of death. Intuition, Alice Bailey said, leads us to the truth as known by the soul, the full awareness of God, the unity of God with man, achievable in rapturous meditation, constant dreaming incantation, and spiritual songs leading to ecstasy, the light. 'The divine self', Helena Blavatsky, the Russian-born spiritualist, wrote, 'could be communicated to the higher spiritual self only in a state of ecstasy'. Ecstasy, according to Plotinus, is 'the liberation of the mind from its finite consciousness, becoming one, and identified with, the infinite'.

Unchecked by Reason, intuition could, of course, connect us with 'God'. Committed to the fearful and fearless abyss of the absolute, it could, however, equally well connect us with all sorts of fundamentalism, from fascism to evangelism, and from subservience to charismatic leaders to holy wars. It can, as Jung said but in a different context, when arguing against the liberation of desire, lead to a 'catastrophe of culture' – in a word 'barbarism'. The danger in such a case is not the irrational, as opposed to the rational, but the anti-rational, often in the form of mass hysteria, which has so often led to an abandoned, unimaginable savagery.

As Blavatsky clarified without losing any of her obscurity, matter is 'the vehicle for the manifestation of soul on this plane of existence, and soul is the vehicle on a higher plane for the manifestation of spirit. These three, matter, soul and spirit, are a trinity synthesized by life which pervades them all'. Indeed, for the New Age, 'one life pervades all forms and those are the expressions, in time and space, of the central universal energy'. The soul, which as Bailey explained, is neither spirit nor matter but the relation between them, the link between God and his form, the consciousness that permeates all substance and underlies all forms, forces matter to assume certain shapes, to become minerals, vegetables, animals and humans. Yet, whatever the shape, the soul of matter, the *anima mundi,* is always present.

All parts of matter, believed to involve consciousness and

human feelings including hunger, aggression and sex which, Carl Jung said, are 'expressions of psychic energy', are, therefore, 'interconnected', part of what the Hindu seer Patanjali, reputed to have lived sometime between 200 BC and 200 AD, referred to as a 'raincloud of knowable things'. The Buddhist doctrine of the *Dharmadhatu*, which means Universal Realm or Field of Reality, explains that there are no dividing boundaries between things and events in the universe – what appear as boundaries are products not of reality but of the way we map and edit reality. Hence every entity in the world interpenetrates every other entity and things are 'related to what they are not'.

Building on this assumption, Rupert Sheldrake, a scientist with a Ph.D. in biochemistry, spoke of a 'morphogenetic field', an invisible matrix or organising field that connects all life and all thought on earth. Austrian-born theoretical biologist Ludwig von Bertalanffy, questioned, on the other hand, the reality of matter. At the subatomic level of quantum physics, matter, he said, dissolves into wavelike patterns of probabilities, which, ultimately, do not represent probabilities of things, but rather probabilities of interconnections. Taking this as his starting point, Austrian-born theoretical physicist Fritjof Capra's 'misty-science' linked Oriental mystical views with quantum mechanics and doubtfully, to say the least, concluded that the whole universe appears as a dynamic web of inseparable energy patterns, each particle of which can be understood only as an integrated part of the whole. The world accordingly is seen as an organism, alive and animated, literally describable as possessing Reason, emotion and a 'world-soul'. James Lovelock, the independent scientist and inventor, took this dogma into ecology, Gaia being seen as a complex organism whose unity is as fragile as that of any living thing.

Of a pantheistic nature and, therefore, devoid of any specific religious connotations, the New Age, like the Gnostics and their philosophers, the Neoplatonists, makes no distinction between God and the world. Unlike the religious orthodoxies which have placed God apart from man, God for the mystics is within. The One and the self are, indeed, identical. For Blavatsky, 'all souls are one with the oversoul', and for Plotinus, our soul, 'divinely possessed and inspired', is identical to the divine mind. This is how the New Age understands the term 'holism', the union of the individual's soul with the 'oversoul'. The real self, according to the Hindus, is 'identical to the ultimate Energy of which all things in the universe are a manifestation' – the identity with God is the supreme identity of the individual, all other identities, including that with our body or intellect, being an illusion.

Connecting with the 'supreme', thereby attempting, as M. Scott Peck, the San Francisco-based author of several spiritual books, said, to be in harmony with the unseen order of things, means connecting with eternity, which, I imagine, must look something like London's Golders Green though probably twice as exciting. As boring as the frivolities supposed to be uttered by the spirits of the dead when summoned by odylic force to our presence, life for the New Age, has, melancholically, only one purpose: the full identification with the divine, the unfoldment of consciousness, or the revelation of the soul. Reality is waiting in vain for the hands of the deconstructed individual to move to her eager breasts. Freedom to be, which would have been the purpose of life if its definition had been entrusted to deers or sparrows, does not feature in its picture, so humanly inhuman.

It follows that emotional desire and sexual attraction is man's 'great illusion'. 'When man was purely animal', Bailey explained, 'no sin was involved. When to this urge was added emotional desire, then sin crept in'. Taking a calculated sin to bed in the hope of finding a shortcut to ecstasy is not the way taught by Bodhidharma, the 28th Indian Buddhist Patriarch who sat in front of a white wall in meditation for nine years. This was not the style of the Stylites and Dendrites, either, who, saints by trade like the yogis of India, turned on by masochism, had condemned themselves to perpetual immobility. A man's life needs, apparently, to be sacrificed like a moth to the flame. This being the case, beauty is immoral, humour a sin, thinking an illness. The walls of the universe contain only silence, the huge silence of the empty eternity, the very voice, as the Tibetan monks hold, of the Great Spirit. Mysticism, one might say, knows everything about life except how to enjoy it. When it rains soup, it goes out with a fork.

Having contacted the 'invisible reality' through the power of intuition, the New Age, or at least its fundamentalist wing, following in the steps of Pseudo-Dionysius, the most important Neoplatonist after Plotinus, identified its citizens, the angels, or what the East calls devas, to which it has given a hierarchical structure. At the top sit the archangels followed by regional officers, guardians, elementals and much more. The elementals, we have been informed, were the 'factor X' in the growth of those huge vegetables in Findhorn's gardens. William Bloom, a co-founder of London's *Alternatives* which has provided a platform for New Age thinking, likewise, told us of his profound experience of the great deva who overlights London and is related to Athena, protector of classical Athens. If the impossible is true, this can, of course, be possible. As true in this sense may also be Bailey's claim that the evil in this world is represented by the Dark Force which is ruled by six oriental and six occidental leaders, or the claim of an acquaintance of mine who assured me she was possessed by 'an evil astral entity' before she was possessed by the evil spirit of Attila, the ant.

As in all occult work, the *a priori* and uncritical acceptance of the 'cosmic truth' is the precondition for all interpretations of our world. The argument, Bailey held, must be considered from the universal to the particular, from the cosmic to the individual. One has to accept uncritically, in other words, that she herself is one of the six 'Masters' sent by the 'Head of the Hierarchy' just before His 'Second Coming' to be shown, as she promised, on TV. Poet Christian Morgenstern Von Korf's Daynightlamp which 'at one flick of the switch turns day, however bright, to blackest night' is floodlighting our path.

The New Age's belief in reincarnation, the cyclical manifestation of lives, the recycling of souls, is at the core of its convictions. Through it, man unfolds his consciousness until it flowers forth as the perfected soul and merges in the greater consciousness of which it is a part. This spiritual development proceeds through many lifetimes, in each one of which the *karma*, set off in our previous lives, being the aggregate of *Skandhas*, the attributes of the old personality, determines the individuality of the new person, his or her character, abilities and problems. Hence some people go to therapy to heal past life traumas just as Christians go to church, that therapeutic institution which John Chrysostom, 'the greatest preacher ever heard', called a 'spiritual hospital', to heal the traumas of this life.

Karma also determines our allotted place in life in some godly preordained order of things – some of us are born to serve the food at banquets and others to enjoy it. Some are, likewise, destined by the law of racial karma to rule, while others are trained to be ruled, exploited and killed. 'The law of racial karma', Alice Bailey wrote in 1949, i.e. long after the horror of Hitler's concentration camps had been exposed, 'is working and the Jews are paying the price (for evil done in past lives), factually and symbolically'. The Jews, her Tibetan guru had communicated to her, 'are the reincarnation of spiritual failures or residues from another planet'.

The princes and the bosses, as Blavatsky proved after she authenticated the various guises under which Count St Germain had appeared on earth, are reborn as princes and bosses. First, 50,000 years ago, she said, Count St Germain was a high priest of the Violet Flame Temple, and then he reappeared as the Old Testament's prophet Samuel before turning into Joseph, the mortal father of Christ. His next manifestation was as St Alban, who was beheaded by the Romans, as Proclus, the most prominent Gnostic of the Athens School, as Merlin, the magician and adviser of King Arthur, as Roger Bacon, the philosopher-monk, and then as Christopher Columbus, Francis Bacon, the prophet of the dawning scientific revolution, and possibly as Shakespeare before turning into Count Saint Germain.

He may have reappeared later as Peter Mandelson, the New Labour politician, but Blavatsky was not there to authenticate it.

Devised by a ruling élite thousands of years ago, the doctrine of karma rejects fully and comprehensively the principle of human equality and theologically justifies exploitation, social hierarchies, even rape, slavery and murder and, of course, the ruthless repression of dissent. The misery and oppression, the humiliation and suffering of the 'outcastes', defined religiously as physically and spiritually contaminating sub-humans, is not due to an atrocious class system but to fate shaped five, ten or, perhaps, fifty thousand years ago, the 'divine hand', past life deeds, the individual's eternal life story, which, although printed in different fonts each time, is responsible for each one's punishments in the life we have. Assuming that reincarnation occurs, it would also be pretty safe to assume that we do not return to earth for pleasure; we fall back on it, instead, like disillusioned satellites.

In India, the caste system, a hidden apartheid claiming legitimacy from the ancient Hindu scriptures, has condemned a quarter of a billion people to lead an utterly degraded life, and Buddhist Tibet still relies on divine guidance. Its problems are ritually addressed by consulting oracles. Slavery is still in force in Buddhist Burma in line, its dictatorship claims, with the Buddhist cultural tradition which, it seems, does not mind narco-capitalism; and Bhutan, run by a Buddhist élite, stands accused, among other things, of ethnic cleansing. Its medieval kingdom has banned democracy, television, blue jeans and other Western influences, observing at the same time all time-honoured traditions of control, including torture.

From a social point of view, Murray Bookchin comments, the Far Eastern understandings have produced a society in which human life is seen from a most passive and resigned perspective, as a steady demographic flow into the 'Sink of Death'. Even divested of their institutional and ideological trappings, they have historically shaped the peasantry into a social body without choice, motivation, respite from, or hope of escaping, poverty. The latter, to which the social hierarchy has condemned them to live, has, instead, been glorified. Even when democracy is proclaimed to be the political system of the country, non-democratic and corrupt practices are the norm. The form has no substance. Man under these conditions really has no choice but to look forward to life beyond life. 'It is natural enough', Byron wrote in Childe Harold's Pilgrimage, 'that those who have so little in this life should look to the next'.

Hence the mystics' 'disinterestedness' in the affairs of this world, their surrender to the status quo. There is no point searching for the truth, Krishnamurti said, since the 'man who seeks truth will never find it', just as there is no point resisting injustice, exploitation, domination or any other trivial and irksome intersections. 'Learn to yield ... let the world take its course and get yourself out of the way of it', is Tao Te Ching's best advice to men and women. No point in collective action, either. Blavatsky tells the faithful to show 'personal' mercy and kindness, 'personal' interest in the welfare of others who suffer, 'personal' sympathy, but, in doing so, to 'act individually and not collectively'. This is, perhaps, in order to ensure that one remains 'a dry leaf without ever at any time having been a green one'. The collective exists only for those working under one master who represents 'the Hierarchy', the superimposed order to which the individual, in the India of Dharma and the China of the Tao, has simply and humbly to bow, in submission, and where possible, in rapturous realisation. The master – in Sanskrit, the guru – freeing the group members from temporal authorities, directs them to the light.

The Western fascination with oriental religiosity, which has as yet to turn into a Broadway musical, marks a return to the 'postmodernist' Hellenistic era of 'anything goes', the time when, as Umberto Eco said, everything Oriental became fashionable especially if it was incomprehensible.

Its path was carved by Madame Blavatsky, a lady nearly related to an earl as Jonathan Swift might have said, in the last quarter of the nineteenth century. A Russian, who in 1875 established the

Theosophical Society in New York, Blavatsky mixed Christian, Jewish and Islamic mysticism with Hinduism, Taoism, and Buddhism. Her work was completed by Alice Bailey who, to borrow the elegant sentence of British poet Charles Causley, 'incapable of surmounting her ferocious goodwill', presented the world over a period of thirty years in the first half of the twentieth century with eighteen books. They were dictated to her, she said, telepathically by Djwhal Khul, a Tibetan master. Jiddu Krishnamurti, the Indian spiritual leader who broke ranks with the Theosophical Society, later made his own major contribution to New Age thinking.

Much of the respectability the New Age has gained is, however, due to psychoanalyst Carl Jung, who, in turn, has a debt to the alchemists whose 'uninterrupted intellectual chain back to Gnosticism gave substance to (his) psychology'. He was also influenced by the Chinese concept of Tao as well as Buddhism and Hinduism. An essential part of his work is, as a result, a mixture of psychology and mysticism, particularly as he claimed to have several times experienced revelation of the divine. One night, he wrote in his memoirs, he saw the figure of Christ on the Cross. His body was made of greenish gold. This he interpreted as an expression of the life-spirit, the *anima mundi*, which has poured itself into everything, even inorganic matter, in metal and in stone.

To these mixtures, other contemporaries have since been adding ingredients according to taste taken from other mystical traditions, those of the Kabbalists, Druids, Essenes, Sufis, Knights Templar, Rosicrucians, Freemasons and others whose secrets have been closely guarded through the centuries. The postmodernist 'anything goes' is in full swing; and, since mysticism decries the employment of our critical faculties in deciding whether to accept its claims, it is up to our blind inner self to point the way.

Though able to absorb the message of the Eastern mystics as much as water can absorb the images it reflects, the West is still searching to find in it some meaning. The search is in direct proportion to the disenchantment with our materialistic, technocratic culture and its values, a response to the vacuum at the heart of modern life. 'Anguish makes even crime and gangs forgivable means of escape', Lorca had rather too munificently observed. But Western spirituality has considerably toned down the features of its Eastern counterpart. The idea of running Europe as a caliphate or a pharaonic kingdom, Joseph Campbell said, had no future even at the apogee of the clergy's power.

The unity of God with man, achievable through rapturous meditation, often constant repetition of the name of God, and spiritual songs leading to ecstasy, is not likely to appeal to more than a handful of western individuals. Even more unappealing are the teachings of Blavatsky, Bailey, Krishnamurti and their followers who insisted that the path of the spiritual man is that of self-denial and self-sacrifice. However, rather than Calcutta where Mother Teresa had chosen to go, in 1969 Jiddu Krishnamurti settled in California. The idea that 'you personally do not count' has nothing to recommend itself to the hypertrophic Western 'I'. These discommodities apart, Eastern religiosity, interpreted by postmodernism and understood according to individual predilections, suits, however, western individuality perfectly well. Something like spiritual Thatcherism – when he was still cardinal Ratzinger, Pope Benedict XVI called it 'spiritual auto-eroticism' – it serves our so unique Iness, often too small for our size; and the problem then is no longer how the perfected soul will merge with the greater consciousness of which it is part, but what it will wear for the occasion.

Deepak Chopra, the New Age guru often quoted by the enlightened élite of the information age in the Upper Class compartment of a Virgin flight to Los Angeles, made the point brilliantly. Individuals, he said, unfolding 'the divinity within', will be able to 'create money and affluence', 'unlimited wealth and abundance'. 'The Age of Aquarius' assertion that the world is about to move away from its materialistic goals is thrown unceremoniously out of the window. Capitalism takes from the mystics whatever it can only to transform it ruthlessly into another commodity, another means of instant gratification, another path to material empowerment. The God of the mystics transformed itself within no time into the God of the High Street in the company of Hollywood's werewolves, vampires and ghosts, some of which seem pretty wealthy if one can judge by their shrouds. The human spirit, though comatosed, is still doing very well on life-support.

The contemplation of the infinite becomes, thus, the 'me' once again, totally self-centred, and also disengaged from what we all call reality. The world out there is not our concern. The homeless to which Deepak Chopra, Wayne Dyer and Chuck Spezzano, the New Age superstars of our time, claim to connect spiritually are left on their own. None of them suggests, to the relief of their audience, that we should do something about the crumbling democratic institutions, the Palestinians or the poor.

'Detached observers', disinterested, we just watch because, as Corinne McLaughlin and Gordon Davidson argue in *Spiritual Politics*, 'perhaps, some of the homeless are Souls who inwardly choose to make a major sacrifice to teach us about the inequities of our system'. Bertrand Russell stingingly made the point. 'The mystic', he said, 'becomes one with God, and in the contemplation of the infinite, feels himself absolved from duty to his neighbour'. Disinterestedness is just self-interest on roads full of prosaic certainties. In any case, there is no such thing as duty to your neighbour, for rather than do something to eradicate the ills of this world, we have, instead, to accept things as they are.

We have to 'accept', as Chopra put it, 'people, situations, circumstances and events as they occur ... because the whole universe is as it should be', because we 'must accept the present as it is'. We are not allowed even to judge because everything, including 'tyranny', is as it should be. We are not allowed to have a point of view, either. Judgment, Chopra said, 'is the constant evaluation of things as right or wrong, good or bad'. Evaluating and analysing, in other words using our intellect, which for the New Age, as for all religious orthodoxies, is the cause of our unhappiness, creates 'a lot of turbulence in (our) internal dialogue'.

All we, therefore, need to do is accept everything in silence because 'only then will (we) become light-hearted, carefree, joyous and free'. The process apparently involves the purification of greed, so that we can have absolute, crystal-clear greed, uncontaminated by human emotions which prick our conscience and disturb our eupepsia, and, perhaps, a better reincarnation system. Unaffected by other concerns, the Gucci New Age society of Greece, a section of which I met at a conference in Crete, had no problem in rattling its jewellery to please the One – soul-shopping seems to be as popular as shoe-shopping or buying aromatic oils for the afterlife. On the other hand, New Agers have no problem giving their support to the status quo. 'There is a role for the right use of destruction', McLaughlin and Davidson argue in their book *Spiritual Politics*, for war, thought 'often the least effective' form of change, can be 'used against rigid and crystallised forms of thought and cultural patterns that prevent life evolving to its next step'. This was how the beloved all-weather precision-guided missiles, smart bombs and stealth technology used by the Americans against the Iraqis received the blessing of the New Age.

Others do not exist. The New Age, Donald Reeves, the former Anglican rector of St James, Piccadilly, which hosts the New Age Alternatives programme, said, 'is not really bothered about community'. Self-indulgent and narcissistic, it needs, William Bloom, an inspiration behind Alternatives, argued, to ground itself 'into social awareness'. A socially aware New Age is, however, an oxymoron. Objective reality, lost in the fog of our interpretations of it, does not exist. There is, consequently, nothing to be aware of, and nothing else we can relate to, apart from the mystical One and the One we all know better, our own selves.

The New Ager's only real problem, often an obsessive preoccupation, is, thus, how best to use the various sophisticated New Age techniques 'to get what you really want' within the realm of this supposedly non-existent reality.

'Remember', Chopra said, 'you are not reacting to the person or the situation, but to your feelings about the person or the situation' – reality is only our interpretation of it. If we want a change, all we have to do is reinterpret this reality in a way that suits our taste, leaving behind what we do not like, all 'negative thoughts'. The latter include whatever we think or feel about the destructive shame and rage of a whole civilisation and our responsibility for it. Confronting war, poverty, racism or manipulation, takes us to the domain of negativity which, it is said, forms a dark cloud in the electromagnetic aura of the Earth and reinforces this negativity. People, rich enough to buy the rarest diseases, can certainly do without such dark clouds.

Instead, we become focused on our own goals: unlimited prosperity, perfect health, total well being. All designed to bring us in touch with pure consciousness which is our spiritual essence, they are provided on a cash and carry basis during an organised descent of some released souls to earth or a weekend workshop by Louise Hay, the Californian metaphysical teacher and head of Hay House, Inc. Enlightened enough, we can then reform not only our personal reality, but even the objective reality which we have sometimes no choice but to acknowledge.

Denounced by Marcuse as a conformist slogan which leaves behind the dark realities in favour of the yuppie dream, 'positive thinking', the purpose of life in the 'schoolhouse of the soul', is the total negation of true spirituality in its own very name. It denies the flesh and blood of human experience, it disengages the individual from reality itself, and separates the inseparable: the yin from the yang, the black from the white, the day from the night. Good without evil is logically impossible, Chrysippus, the Stoic credited with the authorship of seven hundred and fifty books, said more than two thousand years ago; and Jung advised: To discover the deeper source of our spiritual life 'we are obliged to struggle with evil, to confront the shadow, to integrate the devil'. Unfortunately, the life of man, as Bertrand Russell maintained, 'is a long march through the night, surrounded by invisible foes, tortured by weariness and pain, toward a goal that few can hope to reach, and where none may tarry long'. The New Age is not impressed.

The adoption by Occidental individuals of Oriental beliefs is, however, anything but uncritical when self-interest is involved. Indeed, the Westerner enjoys the freedom from the restrictive modernist tradition that makes possible the consumption of quarter-pounders of Oriental 'Ageless Wisdom'. But he or she remains very eclectic when it comes to shopping in the global spiritual supermarket for the best religious beliefs. Oriental concepts are processed by the postmodernist culture industry before entering the market. The new postmodernist religiosity, personalised, 'democratised' as someone dared to say, perfumed and undemanding, is addressed to the individual and intends, like any other product, to meet his or her needs. Sarah Ferguson, the Duchess of York, one of the most prominent New Agers, summed up the superficiality and shallowness of the age's *zeitgeist* on her chat show: 'I personally take a lot of my beliefs from a lot of different faiths', she said; 'it's like making a cake'.

The cake's basic ingredient is invariably the ancient spiritual traditions which are raided in search of wisdom, which is then distorted and adjusted to meet the expectations of the spiritual consumer. Some times the practice is imported in a raw, unpolished manner. A large New Age conference I attended in Sweden was closed by the native American chief, a shaman, with the advice not to go away with 'negative' thoughts: 'Don't', he said, 'because the spirits will be after you'.

The exploitation of ancient spiritual traditions often serves crude commercial interests. Gandhi as a guru, purveying the Wisdom of the East, was appropriated by Apple Mac, which urged us, like he did, to 'think different'. 'Double-click on this icon', Salman Rushdie, the Indian-born British novelist, caustically remarked, 'and you opened up a set of "values", with which Apple plainly wished to associate itself, hoping they'd rub off: "morality", "leadership", "saintliness", "success", and so on'. Gandhi is up for grabs. 'He has become', Rushdie said, 'abstract, ahistorical, postmodern, no longer a man in and of his time but a free-floating concept, a part of the available stock of cultural symbols, an image that can be borrowed, used, distorted, reinvented, to fit many different purposes, and to the devil with hypocrisy and truth'.

The same can be said about One to One which shamelessly used and abused the image of Martin Luther King, or Smirnoff vodka which appropriated Che Guevara's photo by Alberto Diaz Gutierrez to promote its 'spicy' vodka campaign. 'The use of the image of Che Guevara to sell vodka', Gutierrez said just before he died with his bills unpaid, 'is a slur on his name and memory'. The revolutionary hero did after all die in combat with the forces of international capitalism. As Ian Mitroff, a well-established academic who surveyed a clutch of multinational companies which have introduced 'spiritual values' in their practices, concluded: 'A spiritual focus could be the ultimate competitive advantage'. 'Spirituality' is just another means to the same old ends.

Mysticism visits us through the centuries at regular intervals – and when it does, the clock always strikes midnight. So does the rise of fundamentalism – Islamic, Jewish, Christian and Hindu – described by some religious scholars as a Fourth Great Awakening similar to the religious revivals in the 1740s, the early 19th century and the 1880s.

As in the Hellenistic era, individuals, cosmically despairing and politically impotent, look for support and comfort elsewhere, beyond their current experiences, in life after life, which the religious orthodoxies are able or, as in this instance, unable to provide. The Church, though bitterly opposed to the new 'heretics', has made its own generous contribution towards their cause. Concerned about the truth no less than the CIA, and committed to the preservation of its powers, it has rendered meaningless the message it ostensibly conveys.

The living God has become the abstract God to whom lip

service is paid in the places of worship, the absent God who cares nothing about anything. 'It's God', Tasos Leivaditis, the Greek poet, said referring to the God of Christianity, 'because only God doesn't respond'.

Withdrawing from the pains of this world, the New Age, like the Gnostics of earlier times, does not reduce its tensions. But, on the other hand, it does not increase them, either, as all those flying on the new wave of religious anti-modernist revivalism, do to the delight of a madness we know so well that we can recognise it from behind. It is this madness which, if there is something cyclical in the way the world evolves, can, perhaps, in these years of the big wind, lead to a new wave of religiousness that will sweep the planet and spiritually comfort those denied comfort anywhere else.

The shadow is already cast, the word is in the growling of the wind. Rather than a force of resistance, as it once was, capitalism, given its rampant materialism, immorality and cynicism, feeds its growth generously, instead. The time to steer the boat back, as in the Renaissance, within the boundaries of Greece's legend has already come.

Part III: The Spring Depends on Us

1. An Unnameable Essence

The anarchic spirit of the sixties gave way in the seventies to a conformism dictated primarily by harsh economic necessities. Recession cut so deep that there was nobody around to borrow a sixpence from or mug. Certainties decayed, confidence cracked and forms lost their outlines. Survival and its small change philosophy became, instead, the currency of the day. But history did not end. The human spirit did not give up the ghost. Like Prometheus, 'still fettered, still unconquered, still in pain, bold in (their) hope and steadfast in (their) right', as A.D. Hope, the Australian poet, asseverated, people, the unreconstructed individuals, held their ground and affirmed their humanity against all odds. Ethical socialism, not as the programme of a political party providing for nationalisation of the means of production which should have been seen only as a means to an end and not an end in itself, but as the essence of humanity's conscience, an affair of the heart, the socialism which William Morris developed in opposition to utilitarianism, had anything but run out of steam.

Yet the world had entered into a new era, the postmodernist, in which the feminist movement, this broad and quarrelsome coalition, was among the first to challenge the system. By doing so, the feminists achieved more in the last quarter of the twentieth century than women had achieved for ages, or, at least, since Menelaus urged the Greeks to punish the Trojans 'otherwise nobody could henceforth be sure of his wife's safety'. In spite of its success, feminism has not, however, affected in the least the priorities and values which have brutalised our world.

Women, tired of being treated by men as a golf course or as their property, fed up with waiting, as Seferis would say 'on the stone of patience for a miracle', revolted and successfully challenged hierarchies, discrimination, all the perceptions which reduced them to ephemeral pleasure objects, embroiderers, workhorses or respected mothers. Unless they are Baywatch recruits, they still do not earn as much as men, and, although the number of women rising through the ranks is increasing, they still find it difficult to crack the 'glass ceiling' and move into the boardroom. But the balance of power between the two sexes, attitudes and relation patterns, has changed dramatically. 'Soft, gentle and low voice', once 'excellent in women', as Shakespeare thought, is no longer a requirement. The rise of women, novelist Jane Smiley said, is now 'a done deal', and feminism is as outmoded as the suffragettes. Not even a huge seismic movement could make the present repent its investment in equality and fairness. Demanding two incomes to ensure the survival of a small unit, capitalism has probably made sure of it.

On a global scale the feminist movement's achievements look less impressive. Women, a United Nations Human Development report highlighted, occupy only fourteen per cent of managerial and administrative positions, ten per cent of parliamentary seats and six per cent of Cabinet posts. Economic growth, unlike the sea, which can lift all boats at once, has proved insufficient to reduce discrimination against women. Capitalism, someone said, does not raise all boats. It raises all yachts.

The women's march forward is nevertheless beset with problems. In the first place, striving for equal rights without challenging the values of the system and the culture which produces domination, women are discovering the limitations of their goal. 'Capitalism', novelist Fay Weldon pointed out, 'crept in, and cunningly turned women as well as men into wage slaves; the employer is genderless'. Women employers, no less 'averse to change or banknotes', have made no changes in the rules of the game. Women in their employment are still paid less. A woman Prime Minister in the UK changed nothing in terms of existing gender power relations, and one hundred women in the House of Commons have contributed no more to the cause of feminism than the bishops of the Chalcedon Oecumenical Council. Having adopted 'a tone elaborately low', as Wordsworth might say, they are as guilty as their male counterparts of running Tony Blair's pretty tamed parliament. Like the Amazons, whose customs prohibited them from finding a husband before killing a man in battle, many women have, meanwhile, contributed just as much to the brutalisation of human nature which feminism opposes. Navy Lt Demi Moore in *GI Jane*, although the product of the male backlash against female arrogance, eloquently made the point.

Women, Luce Irigaray, the Belgian linguist and Lacanian analyst, held, defined by the lack of something, this something being a phallus, the signifier of an absence, have to stage their own revolution. Hence she championed a new kind of feminism which attributes to the vagina a status equal to the penis, albeit without the latter's personality problems. Like Godot's continuing absence is ever present in the play, the penis' absence is obviously essential to the very structure of the human drama - and to any interpretation attached to it. But as a result, women, forced to find ways to make up this 'symbolic deficit', tried to fit into the male culture and assume, as Carole Pateman, the British political theorist, said, a male identity. Disavowing their bodies and imitating men they, thus, ended up adopting the 'male' attributes of toughness and single-mindedness, speaking and acting like men.

Pateman did not see the disavowal of female identity as a means of bridging the 'symbolic deficit'. The deficit is seen, instead, as a consequence of women's effort to gain citizenship as members of the civil body politic, which is still fashioned after the image of the male 'individual'. But in so doing liberated women, members of the association of Rights Unlimited, looking for 'wetter water' if I can borrow a line from Rupert Brooke, the Romantic English poet, helped as much as men to honour the laws of accumulation, perpetuate the culture of greed, and upgrade the dehumanisation of life. Those few who have broken the 'glass ceiling' are completely indistinguishable from their male counterparts in the pursuit of power and wealth in the interests of 'me'.

Becoming honorary men, dressing up as men to play Prince Orlofsky, does not look likely to take women far on the road to their destiny. This is not going to be achieved by their doing what men ought not to be doing. 'After thirty years of feminism', Germaine Greer, the rebellious Australian thinker, following the conflict in the Gulf, wryly commented, 'women of the rich world killed women and children of the poor world'. I am not sure, as she was not, if this is progress.

Looking for the differences between the sexes is anathema to several hardcore feminists. Such differences are, for them, the expression of a socially-constructed mode of behaviour rather than of our innate nature. Yet people walking in the street, even if dressed the same, as they often are, give a hundred gender signals easily recognised by everybody. A woman does not need to flutter her lace handkerchiefs to be recognised as a woman. But is this social conditioning or nature? Women are supposed to be the guardians of virtues such as warmth, naturalness and gentleness, more intuitive and less competitive, more nurturing and less interested in ideas not relating to their experiences, more social and communicative and less aloof and taciturn. They are, Euripides said, 'readier than men to tell their grief'. Is this true or just an 'oppressive' myth, expressing humankind's erroneous assumptions?

The nature of a woman's 'essence', unnameable and inexpressible, as Julia Kristeva, the Bulgarian feminist theorist, pointed out, is up to the women themselves to define through a poetic language which creates a range of new understandings. But the difference, thankfully, exists. Rather than ignore it, defy and distort their nature, even deny biology, rebel against their having been born as women or even hate themselves for it, women might, therefore, be better off acknowledging it, coming to terms with it, honouring it and celebrating it.

Egalitarian feminism has exposed women to the brutality of the system without giving them a *de facto* equality to men. Even if married, they need to work to help the family, obliged at the same time to take care of the children and the house. In fact, measured in hours, women worldwide spend an average of two-thirds of their working hours on unpaid work, unrecognised as it has no monetary value. The women's liberation army seems to have sunk into a new misery, the lingering testaments of which are very long hours of work, a boring life, powerlessness, despair and depression, which appear to be much more common in women than men.

This state of affairs, equality without quality, is highlighted particularly by the high-flyers, who, unable to resolve the tension between the claims of the self and the claims of the child, to reconcile a career with motherhood and housework, feel they have lost control over their lives. The early and heavy emphasis placed on equality in the workplace is, thus, being questioned.

Frustrated at the difficulties, including men's unwillingness or inability to meet their expectations, radical feminists, those who have never learnt, like novelist Jill Neville, to adore men objectively, raised at the same time a wide range of other issues. Sexual harassment at work was one of the earlier ones. Their campaigns, inflexibly angry, were often conducted with such violence that at times it seemed optimistic to imagine that a man would not end up in jail for his thoughts. Other radical feminists excluded men from important decisions, such as abortion, which, they claimed, were a 'woman's subject'. This, too, has been contested. Gender boundaries are irrelevant, indeed reactionary, as they turn one sex against the other rather than bring the two together in what is an all inclusive effort for a better life.

As E. Annie Proulx, the Pulitzer Prize winning novelist, argued, there are no pure 'women's subjects' in this world. 'Those usually named', she said, 'are intimately and inseparably entwined with the lives of men (sometimes *via negativa*), and to remove men from the equation is a distortion and reduction of the human condition'.

Others endorsed a suprematism which privileged women over men cognitively and morally, considered men superfluous to family life and reduced fatherhood to an emission in a test-tube. The same suprematism endorsed lesbianism as a weapon in the 'war' between the sexes to be carried on in its current form until the arrival of the next bomb designed to kill males only. Other women's groups denounced almost with the same venom incestuous sexual abuse in childhood, which, they claimed, explains all the inequalities under which women labour. Science did not escape the radicals' ferocious attack. Science's choices, Luce Irigaray claimed, are determined by the sex of the scholars involved. Fluid as opposed to solid mechanics is underdeveloped because solidity is identified with men and fluidity with women.

Several of these approaches have retired unobtrusively; and gender politics has run out of steam. Too much *Kyrie Eleison* causes constipation. But what the American feminist critic Elaine Showalter called the *fin de siècle* epidemic of hysteria, banking on the human propensity to paranoia, still remains a force. This hysteria has gone hand in hand with a new puritanism, which, as author Erica Jong said, is not a choice but a compulsion. Fearful of their own sexuality, women, she argued, have ended up advancing ideas of asceticism and sexual morality in an unholy alliance between the radical feminist left and the Bible-thumbing right. The unappealing image of this kind of feminism, Natasha Walter, one of the charismatic feminists of the younger generation, wrote in her book *The New Feminism*, alienates not just men, but also young women. 'It is associated with man-hating and with a rather sullen kind of political correctness or puritanism' which takes away the spice and piquancy of life. 'Gender feminism', Melanie Phillips, the British writer and journalist, argued, too, has ruined the lives of both women and men.

Irigaray, interestingly enough, speaking of the female 'sexual economy', attempted to find the genuine expression of womanhood in another meaningless lump of meaning which only a few feminists could be accused of understanding. She brought into the picture the divine feminine, witchcraft and sorcery. The development of women, she said falling into a New Age mysticism, is linked to 'cosmic rhythms', expresses 'the irreducible relation of their bodies to the universe', and necessitates a distinctively feminine God, a God of fluidity and transient boundaries, of the amorphous elements, water, earth, fire and air. Reason and rationality for her, as for Mary Wollstonecraft, the British eighteenth century feminist, are the product of the patriarchal society depriving women of their own voice – Rousseau in *Emile* insisted that abstract truths are not for women.

Irigaray's views were, however, rebuked by many women including Michele Le Doeuff, the French philosopher, for whom rationality is not an essentially male quality nor can women's capacities be explained by, or reduced to, their sex. 'All gender roles',

Judith Butler, the influential American radical feminist suggested, too, are just 'an imitation for which there is no original'.

The new feminism which seems to be emerging after all successes and tribulations is more self-confident and assertive, and less willing to see women as the victims of their family, business or male friends and partners. Women, after all, represent in some instances more than half of each year's university graduates, and, despite age distribution and career disruption, earn nearly as much as men. Rallied under the flag of an anti-victimhood campaign, which opposed the brand of rights-oriented sisterhood, this tendency held that no woman is a victim unless she wants to be a victim. The huge gap between women and men, the argument goes, is no more.

Yet, as Judith Butler wrote, 'feminism is in a mess'. On the one hand women agree that a more substantial equality is needed, but, on the other, 'when we make room to consider what we mean and how we might act, we are confronted quite quickly with the difficulty of the terms we use'. This difficulty has less to do with social action and more with women's personal life – dealing with loneliness, finding partners, relating to men, preventing them leaving for younger women, and above all pursuing an often elusive dual career as professionals and mothers.

Going beyond the old Left and Right visions of feminine life, Danielle Crittenden, a Canadian writer and one of new feminism's most articulate exponents, took, like Melanie Phillips, another direction. Many women, she held, more than the media would have us believe, rather than try to combine both children and work, would stay home to take care of their children on a full-time basis. Indeed, and if contemporary fiction is a reliable guide, women's focus is still man-centred – man equals fate, as in Lionel Shriver or Alison Pearson's novels before it becomes children-centred, the rearing of 'free-range children', as in Fiona Neill's novels. Women seem as preoccupied with their relation to men as the female characters in Jane Austen's world. 'It's as if feminism never happened', a female journalist commented.

A new realisation that seems to be gradually emerging acknowledges that the dual-career marriage model does not exactly work; and a growing number of women seem to think that raising happy and well-adjusted children is more essential for stability and happiness than competing with men and breaking glass ceilings. At least in the UK, three out of four women opt, indeed, for personal fulfilment rather than a career, which goes a long way to explain why less than five per cent of senior management are women. Incidentally, ranking women against the traditional male career model and then concluding that they have failed to make it to the top is a conclusion as bright as the illation that before women got the vote we had no nuclear weapons.

The crucial issue here is the incompatibility between the job women have been given by nature, to bear children and take care of them for a period of time after their birth, with the requirements of the public sphere. This is what Carole Pateman called 'the separation of civil society from women'. Women cannot reconcile the demands made upon them by two bosses, nature and their employer, neither of whom is willing to give in. Some choose to delay pregnancy for as long as possible, which can cause problems such as infertility and misery or even breast cancer – hormone replacements can make matters worse. And this is what makes the high flyers in particular, those who intend to seize control of the world's weather, angry at both nature and also men, the latter on account of their unwillingness to take responsibility for childcare and housework.

In a cul-de-sac, a number of women choose their career in the end. You cannot be both an intellectual and a mother, author Michele Roberts says in her book *Paper Houses* – hence she relinquished her motherhood. My latest figures show that 42 per cent of American female corporate executives and 49 per cent of those earning more than $100,000 a year are, likewise, childless. The rest, the overwhelming majority, try to juggle everything and make sense of life in a world that does not. But the opposition between the public and private sphere remains, and, as its roots are in nature, no one has quite managed to prove how nature can be reformed. Capitalism, together with technology, work on it of course, and the day hard-driving career women will be able to reproduce without sperm or subcontract all pregnancy details to low-income women may not be far off. Would, as a result, feminist writer Naomi Wolf wondered, motherhood be strengthened when the baby becomes part of a market economy in which rich women, 'too posh to push', utilise the bodies of the poor? This is 'a devil's bargain', she decided. Bearing children is certainly an obstacle to a full professional career. But resenting it, resenting nature for its gift, is as dehumanising as anything obsessed with power and wealth.

On the other hand, and as nature cannot be reformed, one cannot conclude that caring for the family is a woman's work or that work and motherhood are incompatible. Such assumptions, gender-based, lead inevitably to discrimination, even if the latter falls outside the anti-discrimination provisions of the law. The law can, of course, be extended to cover even more areas, but any new legislation can backfire and create new kinds of discrimination. In any case, as Germaine Greer wrote, more legislation does 'nothing to make me more at ease with my woman's body'.

Privately, men and women conduct their own negotiations, leading more often than not to genuine misunderstandings as a result of which the feminist movement, generalising, sometimes tends to give men a raw deal; and men do not like it. Much less, of course, do they like the most disagreeable face of feminism, which regards them as thuggish layabouts or absent fathers, the cause of society's ills. Fed-up with all this, the tail chasing its dog, normal men, all those who never read a book, reject as a rule the 'New Man' and, together with it, salads, low-cholesterol foods and weekly sewing parties, and return to their unreconstructed selves.

In most species the male's evolutionary strategy is to try to fertilise as many females as possible, while the female tries to save herself for the finest mate available. It looks as if women will have to save themselves for much longer than they had bargained for.

2. Contradictions Are Our Hope

Civil society re-engaged in the struggle to redefine its moral purpose, assert itself over the market, and win back its power as the chief regulator of social and political developments. Wealth, as Plato argued, cannot be allowed to have the controlling influence. Engaged through various communication networks, clustered according to themes, in democratic subversion, or what ecosocialist André Gorz called 'imaginative subversiveness', the 'planetary citizens movement' started consistently to raise the themes of the future in order to change the haecceity of society and free the individual from forms enclosed in time. In doing so, in proving that change can originate at grassroots level despite opposition from the top, it also educated our culture, and contributed significantly to its transformation.

As it has often happened, standards arise, not from institutions or politicians who have lost much of their capacity to regulate, order and control society from above, but from each new generation's 'flaming new songs' emerging when time reaches new crossroads. Hegel made the point a long time ago when he said that social change is the fruit of disharmony between the state, civil society and ethical values. Social stability in such a case cannot be regained unless readjustments are made; and what is expected to change is the system itself, its institutions, because institutions are the main area under the direct influence of man.

New ethical concerns relating to sexuality, gender issues, minorities and the way modernism deals with the environment emerged as instantaneously as the first lines of Rilke's elegies, which, according to the story, were heard in the wind when he was walking on the rocks above the sea. More issues were raised in connection with human rights, the treatment of animals, genetically engineered food, intensive livestock farming and the corporations' unscrupulous exploitation of natural resources.

The new spirit of resistance, often obstreperous, to the onslaught of the market was also evident in the effort to force the multinational corporations to stop shifting their factories around the globe in order to take advantage of cheap labour, lax environmental standards and the source of child labour. It was the driving force in the mobilisation of public opinion against the homogenisation of the global media, entertainment and culture, the greedy individualism of the unfettered markets, the American-style capitalism which threatens to drain Europe's social market economy of its social content, the advancing corrosion of representative democracy, and above all the aggressive projection of imperial US power.

The various intellectual traditions, which met on the battlefield against the disagreeable aspects of globalisation, dealt also with many other issues, including the corporations' drive to pursue nature to all her hiding places and unearth all her secrets primarily through genetic engineering and cloning, those ultimate shopping experiences offered in the biological marketplace with an enthusiasm proportionate to the anticipated capital returns. Cloning which, like Baron Frankenstein's dream to render man invulnerable to any but a violent death, opening the way to a commercial eugenics civilisation, is a frightening new form of biocolonialism in which corporations become the ultimate arbiters of the evolutionary process itself.

The going was never easy as the immense power in the hands of corporations and the media empires ensures nothing changes unless the powerful of this world are powerless to stop it. Even so, the process showed that the possibilities for change are, and will always be, there.

Structures and systems are as ephemeral as the proclivities of the human mind and as vulnerable as its virtues. In spite of their inherent tendency to solidify themselves behind certainties, they are ceaselessly affected by the way people think and daily cut down to size to accommodate the realities visited by the passions of each new generation. Likewise, although relatively enduring, they are also in a state of perpetual fluidity that corresponds to the fluidity of the human mind, its ever-changing attributes, except, of course, that structures are always outpaced and reformed by it. The context, which encompasses everything and is life's moulding force, is, thus, itself endlessly reshaped, and man's autonomy is always there, albeit just like the iridescent bubbles of foam on the seashore that mirror the sun for endless infinite instants.

Likewise, the free market, unlike Christianity or the silent laws of nature, cannot settle on eternal, unalterable, inviolable forms. It is not, therefore, the purveyor of a monolithic ideology. In its drive to sell its products, increase its market share and conquer the hitherto unconquered, it goes unremittingly through a process of continuous transformation. Accommodating frustration, rebellion and conflict, embracing alternative lifestyles and allowing for variety and innovation, it gives the individual a chance to distance himself or herself from the prevailing values. 'Capitalism', Jeffrey Weeks of London's South Bank University said, 'sees no barriers; there are profits to be made from any group of people'. Homosexuality, largely unacceptable until the 1980s, is quite acceptable now, not so much because of some new human awareness but following the recognition of the strength of the 'pink pound'. Gays and lesbians are the ultimate dinks (double-income-no-kids) deserving thereby the ultimate capitalist respect.

A certain degree of autonomy, personal and social, is further preserved partly because it helps to generate new ideas, trends and fashions on which capitalism banks, and partly because, being controllable, it is not threatening. The argument, of course, is that in squeezing in a minimal negativity, it only tames, assimilates and co-opts the dynamics of negation and change in order to control, distort and neutralise it. Punk, this rebellious, anarchic, anti-authoritarian, often nihilistic movement of the 70s, was assimilated into the fashion industry before history could blink its eyes. But equally true, the culture industry and its manufactured realities cannot survive on routine. Taboo breaking is practically mandatory – even the surrealists, those 'fools' who attacked modernism from the outer limits of reality, have been appropriated by an industry happy to market scentless perfume. Contemporary societies, on the other hand, are both latitudinarian and repressive, hedonistic and puritanical, democratic and authoritarian, and people, with heteromerous sets of views, tend both to conform and to differ.

The culture of those who differ may be that of a minority, but the input of this minority in terms of ideas is abundant. Ideas seem always to emerge just like new teeth waiting to burst out of the gums of a child. Business, for its part, is only too happy to accommodate them, and dissidents, if they become numerous enough, can affect the type of choices society makes. In spite of institutional rigidity and many almost instinctive cultural reactions, their pro-active rather than reactive social action can make quite a difference. This process, which is a condition of development and growth, can, however, and does sometimes go, as the American cultural theorist Douglas Kellner pointed out, for an implicit or even explicit critique of capitalism and the existing order of things. Never entirely identical with itself, self-critical and self-destructive, unable to overcome its inherent inbalances which globalisation has only highlighted, the system remains subject to dislocation.

Contradictions are in its nature, and 'contradictions', Bertolt Brecht asserted, 'are our hope'. In the early hours of a moonless night, when the 'window of opportunity' opens, a crack team of insomniac radicals may well then be able to break through. The probable and improbable are not territories whose frontiers are heavily guarded by an army. As Agathon, the tragic poet, put it, 'many things happen contrary to probability'. One such thing has been the growing popular backlash against globalisation that is sweeping both rich and poor countries alike to the dismay of both the pro-free market governments and corporate executives.

Following the September 11 crisis or rather the US loss of perspective in dealing with it, the movement inadvertently known as the 'anti-globalisation movement' was forced to readjust its policy. The ferocious American reaction to the desperate plea of the wretched that is incomprehensible to those living in 'the land of the free and the home of the brave', overshadowed all other concerns. Peace in a very turbulent world, threatened by a re-energised fundamentalism, both religious and political in both the US and the Muslim countries, offering solutions at once absolute, definite, unequivocal, durable, unrefined and darker than darkness itself became the priority of the day. Indeed, the pre-September concerns appeared for a while to be on the other side of beyond. The story did not, however, have a happy ending, for the antiwar majority in the pro-war countries failed to influence government policy despite the latter's flagitious nature.

It seems that, though absolutely free to choose whom and what we like, Nicholas Cage or Michael Douglas, a Skoda Roomster or a Suzuki Supermini, a good time out or dinner in with the wife, trivialities such as war and peace are none of the citizens' concerns. People are free to do their shopping in the global supermarket but they are not allowed to challenge the hegemony or counter the power, of all those who manipulate their desires, direct their choices and in effect decide on their behalf. This is our normality whose abnormal condition, like the abnormal condition of every abnormal person, the world cannot even see.

Manipulated by their representatives, excluded from the political process and disempowered, many opted temporarily out of politics – perhaps, for a snack. Some, those who, like Marshal Cambronne, who when invited by the British to surrender, articulated his anger for all time with the single word *Merde*, were lost in the process. But many others took stock of the difficulties and re-evaluated their potential while waiting for the next appropriate opportunity to act. Silence is not the spokesman of the unacceptable. It is not 'the silence of derailed trains'.

The effort to tilt the scales on fairness' side has anything but been abandoned. The antiwar movement has been trying to prevent the 'cosmic conflict' between the insane forces of 'good' and the lunatic forces of 'evil', but it is also striving for Justice, 'the highest prize', Goddess Athene told the Athenians, a state can win. To win it, we need wisdom and also some good luck.

I am not sure how we can acquire the former, but for the latter just copy this book nine times and send it to nine different friends.

3. The Unfinished Business

Embodying the revolt of the civic society, the movement of the Greens broke away from liberalism and Marxism, both of which dissolved nature into a utilitarian order, and viewed its domination as the necessary price of human freedom. Inspired by the Romantic movement of the nineteenth century, they were at first animated by a nostalgic longing for a simpler age, which, they believed, enabled man to live in harmony with nature. Theologically tinted, their initial arguments appealed, thus, to notions of humanity's 'stewardship' of nature. Nature, being God's creation, had to be preserved in His name rather than be destroyed by man. For American Christian naturalist Wendell Berry, the destruction of nature is 'the most horrid blasphemy', for, as he reminded us, God is the landowner and we are here on earth only as His 'guests' and 'stewards'.

Some Greens, the deep ecologists, spoke on behalf of nature itself. They hold that speciesism, akin to racism or sexism, is a blind prejudice which refuses to acknowledge the right of living creatures to live on a par with man. James Lovelock, the British specialist in atmospheric sciences, better known for his 'Gaia Hypothesis' which sees the earth as a living being in its own right, described humans as merely 'intelligent fleas' feeding on the body of Gaia. His mystical nature-worshipping faith, which attributed to humans the same 'intrinsic worth' possessed by cockroaches, was denounced for degrading the human spirit. As objectionable to the same critics was his giving the job of nature's interpretation to the mystics, those, in other words, who feel qualified to explain nature's 'transcendental essence' which, as they believe, is fused with man's innermost nature.

Another, albeit earlier exponent of this New Age ecophilosophy was Rudolf Steiner, founder of the German Theosophical Society, and later of the Anthroposophical Society. Steiner's educational principles, which freed education from pressure to achieve, and placed the emphasis on feelings rather than understandings, were internationally acclaimed. So was his biodynamic farming, a form of organic agriculture. However, his racial theories, which placed white Europeans at the summit of his human hierarchy, blended seamlessly into the Nazi vision of a dominant Aryan race. Interestingly enough, 'the inferior kinds of human beings', i.e., those who have not reached a 'high level of development', were for Steiner destined by the law of karma to harm the world. 'The laggard souls', he wrote in 1909, 'will have accumulated in their karma so much error, ugliness and evil that they will form, for the time being, a special union of evil and aberrant human beings who oppose the community of good men'. Rudolf Hess, the deputy leader of the Nazi party, had no difficulty joining the Anthroposophical Society, a section of which is still today connected with the German ultra-right.

Deep ecology is in many ways a curious phenomenon, often associated with what has been called 'the modernisation of Fascism'. Its roots are to be found in the mystical tradition initiated in Germany by Meister Eckhart, carried on by the nineteenth century Romantics, and culminating in the 1920's occult and esoteric spiritualist beliefs which blended with romantic nationalism, a racism invoking Kipling's 'white man's burden', and the deification of nature.

In our days, this movement, the 'New' Right, opposes the degradation of the environment by America's technological imperialism, the destruction of national cultures by America's cultural imperialism and the annihilation of the spirit of man by the forces of modernism and, in particular, by soulless American materialism. The destruction of nature, it holds, is life-threatening, not just in a physical, but more importantly in a spiritual sense. Nationalism merges, thus, with antirationalism and esoteric cults influenced by neopagan Germanic, Celtic and Indian religions, and also with a cultural racism. The latter is intended, in the name of 'ethnopluralism', to protect national European cultures against threats emanating from both the US and the Third World.

The German 'Green' national-socialists, warning against 'the increasingly obvious ecological catastrophe', call, thus, for 'a radical revolution in consciousness' that links 'the right to life' with racism, a revival of *völkisch* ideology and a regeneration of 'spiritual' life, which, among other things, will dispel 'the Auschwitz myth'. Rudolf Bahro, the former Marxist philosopher who in the last few years of his life converted to New Age Deep Ecology, actually reconnected with the völkisch ideologies of the 1920s. Believing that Hitlerism was 'among other things an early reading of the ecology movement', he really went as far as to wish for the arrival of a 'Green Adolf', who, as a spiritual leader, would lead the world into ecological salvation. 'A bit of ecodictatorship', he said, 'is needed' to deal with the problems of the day. Murray Bookchin's answer at a seminar held at Berlin's Humboldt University, where Bahro used to teach, was that an 'ecological dictatorship' is a contradiction in terms, an oxymoron.

Just as controversial is what is termed 'shallow ecology', which some refuse even to grace with the word ecology as they see in it nothing more than environmentalism which is contemptuously dismissed. Recycling old newspapers and empty bottles or saving a few owls does not look likely to arrest the ecological crisis caused by the capitalist megamachine and our own insatiable appetites. The case of the conservation movements is made this time in the name of man rather than God or a deified nature, for environmental degradation compromises human interests. Nature, and everything in it which Aristotle thought had a purpose as nothing is created in vain, is valued, but only as a means to the humans' own anthropocentric ends. This bolsters, however, the illusion that everything man encounters exists only insofar as it is his construct. It seems, Heidegger said, as though 'man everywhere and always encounters only himself'.

Even so, Green policies have never been easy to promote, for the public has never been willing to sacrifice its comforts for the sake of a greener, safer world. Environmentally aware citizens hate the polluted air of the cities but they do not want to give up the car, perhaps because, though the world is getting smaller, it takes longer to go to work. They agonise over climate warming but it is 'others' who will have to make the necessary sacrifices – not 'us'. Yet something has changed, enough for the mainstream political parties to appropriate the slogans of the Greens and then campaign for a greener, safer world.

Aware that environmentalism is as good for business as honey from Hymettos is for the connoisseur, politicians and corporations metamorphosed into friends of the earth, the resources of which capitalism continues to plunder in the name of growth. Even companies such as Exxon and Mobil Oil, notorious for their contribution to the galloping ecological crisis, have engaged in a sustained greenwashing, which, however crude, does not fail to make an impact. The false sense of security such a meaningless green agenda has generated in a confused public was the gain of those forces of 'progress' which rely on destruction. André Gorz long ago warned: We must refuse to allow the capitalist managers to take over the critique of growth by appropriating the green vocabulary which only makes sense in reference to a total change. And Ivan Illich summed up the challenge: we either agree to impose limits on technology and industrial production so as to conserve natural resources, preserve the ecological balances necessary to life, and favour the development and autonomy of communities and individuals, or the limits necessary to the preservation of life will be centrally determined and planned by ecological engineers. The choice is simple: 'conviviality or technofascism'.

The Green movement soon faced much more serious challenges. Split between those who see no alternative but to work with the establishment and those who, having no faith in it, stand for a new rainbow grassroots movement, it has lost much of its hostility to the intolerable and also much of its effectiveness. Overall, it succumbed to pragmatism and the political compromises which have been waiting to happen like Christmas. In spite of its refreshing new platitudes, its original radicalism evaporated, and, together with it went the power that fired the imagination of its pioneers. The German Greens, in particular, forced so embarrassingly to compromise over issues such as nuclear energy or road traffic, have lost much of their credibility. The Green party ended up being as good as carbonated water without the sparkle.

Committed to thinking globally and acting locally, other strains of Greens advanced an ecophilosophy which, with varying degrees of emphasis and articulation, can be found in the 'small is beautiful' theme of Fritz Schumacher, the 'liberated zones' of Rudolf Bahro, the 'personal/planet' theme of Theodore Roszak, or in the 'bioregionalism' of Kirkpatrick Sale. Humanity, Sale, the American writer and ecologist, urged, has to model itself on nature, as in the natural world 'nothing is more striking than the absence of any centralised control, any interspeciate domination'. The root ideas of ecocommunalism are that nature's inherent constitution and manner of growth serve as society's regulatory ideal. 'Nature', ecologist Robert Nisbet, echoing earlier Greek beliefs, emphasised, 'is simple for those who understand; society should be also'.

As the threat to the planet emanates, not from gas emissions, but from the people who refuse to control them, the environmental movement, initially concerned about everything but people, started to discover its own limits.

The ecological crisis, veteran author and environmentalist Tom Athanasiou said, cannot be dealt with until environmental and social issues are forcefully and directly linked. 'It is folly to believe', he wrote in his 1998 book *Divided Planet*, 'that a realistic environmental and developmental agenda ... will not be compelled to take up the unfinished business of the old left movement'. For Athanasiou, 'progress' and 'development' have to break with the logic of unlimited growth and measure themselves against the overall human and ecological wellbeing. In various forms and degrees, this is the thesis of the fourth wave of environmentalism.

Borrowing elements from the work of Saint Francis of Assisi, Peter Kropotkin and William Morris, ecocommunalists considered a harmonious relationship between humans and other beings as well as between culture and nature as vital for the future. They also rejected greed and competition, supported decentralisation and freedom from arbitrary authority, coercion or repressive laws, and placed a limpid emphasis on the need for a harmonious balance between mind – body – spirit. Man for them is a part of a larger order with which we have to harmonise our existence.

Ecocommunalism, rather anarchic, rejected the authority of the State and in this it was opposed by ecosocialism. The latter, though it supported the empowerment of the local community, argued that the goal can be facilitated by the State rather than thwarted by it. Democracy, Boris Frankel, the Australian social and cultural theorist, argued, would not even survive the abolition of state institutions. Ecocommunalism found itself at odds with the Green parties, too, as the latter tend not to value the need for a new ecological paradigm and are not concerned with inner invisibilities and awakenings. Establishment figures, seeing in ecocommunalism's dream of an organic community the rejection of pluralism and individual freedom, objected totally to it. One of them, George Soros, the mogul of the financial world, has denounced it as the 'enemy', who, trying to instil unquestioned values, beliefs and rules to link people together, breeds 'intolerance and repression'.

But ecocommunalism, although it was never taken seriously as a practical alternative and kept going huffing and puffing, was able to highlight the human dimension of the ecological problem. Amitai Etzioni's communitarianism that emerged from this realisation attempted to promote some reforms which, it reckoned, the system would be able to endorse without screams of pain.

Communitarianism rejected the concept of individual rights and freedoms without individual obligations that sustain the common good. Amitai Etzioni, the George Washington University Professor who coined the term, urged that society has to move from 'me' to 'we', and, rejecting competition between conflicting individual claims, rely on cooperation and mutual responsibility. To this effect, and as both the State and the market have failed to provide the solution, we must revive the intermediate institutions – family, school, neighbourhood and the wider community, and rely on ourselves rather than the state. The state needs, however, to act along community-friendly lines – it should not be neutral in matters relating to the common good, for a neutral state leaves the door wide open to the market to impose its own values. It does not strengthen the citizens' allegiance to it, either.

The communitarian views, a kind of a moral imperative, were broadly endorsed by Bill Clinton, the US president, and Tony Blair, the British prime minister, albeit with the same conviction they would have endorsed vitaminised toilet paper. But communitarianism, which somehow failed to impress either the young, who were not taken by its absent ebullience, or people old enough to have seen through anything new, faced considerable opposition.

The left rejected it because it does not reduce the structural imbalances of a system dedicated to money – Etzioni himself actually warned after the collapse of his 'Third Way' model that material consumption is not the right basis for personal fulfilment. And postmodernist groups attacked it as representing the white male backlash. Defined by the majority, the postmodernist argument went, it does nothing to help marginalised groups such as women, blacks, ethnic minorities or homosexuals. It was also resisted by individualism on the grounds that it restricts self-determination.

Communitarianism, at any rate, has faded into the background. The batteries that kept the inner light on went flat the moment its apostles confronted free market economics, which American economist Milton Freedman advanced as a policy adviser to President Reagan, and to which the world has adhered blindly for a number of years in repentance for its previous endorsement of interventionist policies. Though the free market has not delivered the goods, for inequality has widened and alienation cuts deeper than ever before, communitarianism did not make it as it did not have what it takes to turn itself into a movement.

As concerned about the disintegration of our communities and its institutions, others advanced the citizenship theory, which, evoking images of classical Athens, called for the active exercise of citizenship responsibilities and virtues. This had to be seen not as a burden, but as an intrinsically rewarding activity, the highest life available as in the Aristotelian model, standing above the pleasures of family, neighbourhood and profession. Some even argued that in this context even private life is antisocial. The concept, which does not challenge the free market and its institutions, rests on trust and the citizens' active participation in public life, a public-spiritedness and also civic virtue, what professor Robert Putnam called 'social capital'. The latter includes tolerance of difference, cooperation, civility, self-restraint and a sense of social justice without which society's ability to function will be diminished. It also requires the citizens' participation in public meetings where decisions can be expected to be reached by consensus or compromise.

But active participation by the citizens in public life has no forums for deliberation. Even so, it was dismissed on the familiar grounds that it would allow the majority to outvote minorities or give a free reign to objectionable 'seabeds' of civic virtue. Such 'seabeds' are the family, often 'a school of despotism', the church, which preaches deference to authority, ethnic groups, known often for their intolerance, or civil society, happy to forego civil virtue if it conflicts with particular interests and goals. Education is even more controversial owing to the unresolved conflict between liberalism and ethnic and religious groups, the latter being described by Canadian political philosopher Will Kymlicka as 'free-riders benefiting from stable liberal order while doing nothing to help maintain it'.

James Fishkin, a political scientist at Stanford University in California, took the concept a step further and tried what he called 'deliberative democracy' in gatherings of representative samples of citizens he organised in Texas, Australia, Denmark, China and lastly in Marousi, an Athens suburb, where he was able to say 'we have seen the ancient past, and it still works'. To some extent this was the path which Ségolène Royal, the French socialist presidential candidate, took when she initiated the 'participatory debates' across France to work out her own priorities except that at the end she was marginalised.

The failure of new theoretical social models to humanise the free market has, however, much less to do with the intellectual force of the arguments advanced and much more with our world's emotional anaesthesia, which nothing short of an operation can end. Plagued by greed, corruption and brutality, its individualistic culture cares about life no more than Gauguin did about all those Tahitian women whom he infected with the syphilis that ravaged his eyesight, his limbs, his intestines and eventually his sanity. It was this realisation, indeed, that brought back onto the streets at the very beginning of the new millennium hundreds of thousands of people, all those who, having crossed the revered bridge of postmodernist silence, were certain as to what, at least, they did not want.

In doing so, they showed character. Society nevertheless has forgiven them.

4. The Unsubmissive

The anti-globalisation movement, which ought to be known as Global Resistance, or even better as the movement for Global

Justice, spread like an Australian bushfire. The world will be saved, as André Gide, the French novelist, put it, if it can be, 'only by the insubmissive', those who are the salt of the earth and responsible only to God whom 'we must achieve'. Once again, it looked as if 'spring', as poet Odysseus Elytis would have said, actually 'depends on us'. But in so doing, in opposing impenitently the pervasive destructive powers of the market and the failure of the political system to represent the forces of resistance to it, this movement has consistently encountered the opposition of the established order which remained uncontaminated by the outbreak of health.

Peaceful expressions of democratic opposition were, therefore, as one might have anticipated, ignored or dismissed just like those salesmen happy to offer a free estimate for a new kitchen. Even the unprecedented antiwar demonstrations failed to win the ear of a political class that crudely serves only its own interests. But 'how could you dream they'd listen', as Yeats might say. For the newspapers, those which appeal even to those who cannot read, they were nonevents which just happened to unfold in the same black rain which hits the windows of their glass-plated offices. Hence the rage of the protesters that is impossible to express. How can you do it? 'Strike nails into the sound barrier, behead dandelions and candles, assert yourself on the couch', as Günter Grass suggested? Maturity, the compensatory gift kindly offered by time to its long acquaintances, had not much to contribute.

Denied an audience, in despair, untamed youthfulness felt the only way to make a point was mindless violence, which incidentally the media themselves have profitably turned into another commodity. Dr Stockmann's advice given in a rather controversial Ibsen play – 'you should never wear your best trousers when you go out to fight for freedom and truth' – seems not to have lost its value over the years. People 'learn a style from despair', as English poet William Empson said. Despite the violence, the protesters were not, however, a force of destruction. All they were seeking was a world in which power is taken away from global corporations and put back where it belongs: in the hands of good, old-fashioned elected representatives of the people. It really sounds simple except that, as someone said copying US president Lyndon Johnson's colourful vocabulary, it is like trying to put the shit back into the horse's arse.

But the exchange rate between philosophising with a hammer, the kind of protest that lacks the civil self-command of the academic classes on the one hand, and results on the other tends to be rather poor. Denounced in fiercely official tones, as it was after the Genoa riots, by British prime minister Tony Blair as 'a travelling circus of anarchists' and by Silvio Berlusconi, the Italian prime minister, as an enemy of Western civilisation on a par with Islamic terrorists, the anti-globalist movement lost part of its appeal. But considering that a 'moderate' is, as Noam Chomsky said, anyone who supports Western power, and an 'extremist' anyone who objects to it, loss of 'respectability' and 'credibility' is, needless to say, as certain as snow in Davos.

Whatever the frustrations, effective opposition to liberal imperialism, corporate greed, global injustice and environmental degradation takes much more than violence on the streets of the First World. Violent opposition confronts the system on all fronts, denying it even the democratic legitimacy it claims. Such opposition, perhaps just the prelude to more serious future intemperance, may pay dividends in the short term. In the long term it is, however, bound to backfire, for the prospect of a world anticapitalist revolution is not on the cards. The 'groups of liberated workers', who, 'once the state is overthrown', would 'group themselves harmoniously together and work like a colony of bees', as Peter Kropotkin, the Russian anarchocommunist, expected, do not seem likely to abandon their television screens to man the barricades. Despite its therapeutic effect on the psyche of the protesters, its purifying effects, violence remains, thus, politically an unattractive proposition. It is not 'wearable', as a modern Greek would say. But it can, nevertheless, be an occasional complement to formally constituted politics, even a welcome deviation from norms if it shakes the establishment out of its somnolence and reminds it that politics is not divorced from ethics.

Opposition to the disagreeable aspects of our situation through established channels, on the other hand, respects the institutional arrangements but it leads at best to inevitable compromises. Hence the nature of critical engagement is always contentious as it can easily lead to the absorption of the opposition by the establishment. But reform, if it is to be on the agenda, cannot stay like an unwanted dog at the system's doorstep. It cannot be contemplated outside national or international institutional frameworks.

This is what the Non-Governmental Organisations, NGOs, are doing. Playing their dedications initially like pirate radio stations, but mature and influential now, they have taken a leading role in expressing civil society's anxieties and also its determination to stand up to the abuses of the system by governments and the corporate world. Governments, hostages of crony capitalism and narrow profit-maximisation, forgetful of their social and political responsibility, detached from everything human in life, pressumed obsolete, and, indeed, in the throws of a crisis of legitimacy, are no longer to be trusted. Hence the lead taken by the NGOs, perceived today by the public as the authentic voice of civil society – the term, which was used by the anti-communist intellectuals of Eastern Europe, became fashionable just before the fall of the Soviet empire. Achieving such a high status, they have partly been helped, as sociology professor Nicos Mouzelis said, by the decline of statism, which has encouraged not only the development of the market, but also the creation of a 'third sector' which functions neither according to profit nor to the state/party logic.

Resented often by both governments and multinational corporations, NGOs have denounced the destruction of cultures, economies, people and the erosion of democracy by the forces of globalisation and streamlined capitalism. They oppose repression, poverty, inequality and discrimination, the ravaging of the environment, corruption and the lack of ethical standards, the exploitation of women and children, illegal exports of armaments or the production of genetically modified organisms capable, one day, of explaining to us exactly what they can do. Their aims, diverse, often take them in contradictory directions. Some of them, indeed, flirt dangerously with the extreme and populist Right which remains rooted in Romantic attachment to yesteryear, mysticism, racism, and hatred of the US and the Jews. Opposition to a system which has gone too far remains, however, the unifying force even if the events of September 11th and beyond have disturbed the preexisting balance.

Some of the NGOs, the first generation of them, which comprises organisations such as *Médecins sans Frontières*, whose co-founder Bernard Kouchner, a former communist who was appointed Foreign Minister by French president Nicolas Sarkozy, and Oxfam, try to help those in need through charitable work. The second generation, which includes groups such as Friends of the Earth and Greenpeace, have set as their task the protection of the planet from commercial and other despoliation, working, if possible, in alliance with governments drained of all sympathy for humanity, business with unformulated guilt syndromes and/or under the auspices of the United Nations. The third generation of NGOs, militant groups such as Globalise Resistance and *Ya Basta*, are the radical edge of the whole movement that views the first and second generation NGOs like those Spartans who, in their campaign against the Tegeans, took along the chains to tie them but they lost the battle and were chained with the chains they had brought.

The radical groups favour, instead, campaigns of civil disobedience and direct action, including sanctions to enforce labour and environmental standards. Sanctions are anathema to both corporations and Third World countries, which are afraid that they may be used only as an excuse for the further curtailment of their exports.

Having chosen cooperation rather than confrontation with the corporations, many of the NGOs have opted for a quiet behind the scenes chat with their representatives in order to take their money for a good purpose. Hence the so-called 'alliances' formed between Greenpeace and Unilever, the consumer goods multinational, Oxfam and Starbucks, the global coffee retail chain, the American Rainforest Alliance and Chiquita, the US banana giant, or Save the Children and American Express. The governmental system, the argument goes, is not delivering through regulatory approaches, so the NGOs are now turning to the market forces as a catalyst of change. The cost of this approach does not seem to matter as long as the price is right.

To look good rather than like engines of destruction, some companies, 'hostages to reputational risks', as someone disapprovingly said, have on the other hand, been offering kind words never heard since the beginning of time and also money for various educational, artistic and charitable projects. Reebok has formed a partnership with Amnesty on human rights, Time-Warner with Time to Read on Literacy promotion, Visa with Reading is Fundamental on Literacy, Nokia with the International Youth Foundation on teaching packs to children with learning difficulties or British Gas with Help the Aged. They all do some nice work albeit often with funds accumulated on the back of 'outrageous profits' – this is what the European Union has called the profiteering by Visa and Mastercard, and various tax avoidance schemes. They are also delighted to subscribe to *Fairtrade*, in which a few seem to have discovered a new source of revenue, and to market new 'ethical' products – spanking paddles made from naturally-felled wood, non-toxic sex toys endorsed by the World Wildlife Fund, and *Fairtrade* bondage gear.

Celebrities, moved by so much sorrow in plain clothes, have joined the party in the same spirit. Angelina Jolie is now goodwill ambassador for the UN High Commissioner for Refugees, Michael Douglas is a UN 'Messenger for Peace', David Beckham, Ricky Martin and Robbie Williams are Unicef's celebrity supporters, Giorgio Armani is associated with UNHCR, Pierre Gardin with

Unesco and so on. The UN Population Fund has no less than five former Miss Universes in its stable of goodwill ambassadors. Seeing celebrities' names associated with good causes rather than expensive divorces, ludicrous hairstyles or ghastly addictions is certainly a step in the right direction. But, as it happens, an act of concern is also good as it enhances the celebrities status, brings cash in the bank through the increased exposure, and gives an illusion of depth to what is often shallow waters. As someone observed, giving to a cause used to be an act of self-denial. Now it is more of a transaction.

A few others, most notably Microsoft co-founder Bill Gates and investor Warren Buffett, the richest and second richest men in the world, have pledged billions of dollars to charities, apparently, to placate, like Polycrates, the all too powerful but enlightened tyrant of Samos, the jealousy of the Gods. Polycrates threw his most precious ring into the deep waters only to recover it a few days later when his cook cut open a large fish freshly caught. Their gesture, which, some believe, heralds what has been described as 'the third golden age of philanthropy', was most generous and will support a few good causes. It does not, however, conceal the fact that by their donations these billionaires appropriate society's duty to act in support of those deserving its support. Nor does it do any good to all those worthy causes which are sidelined by the priorities of the billionnaires. In any case, the British nurses do not need donations from very wealthy footballers to ensure their survival – they need, instead, a decent society aware of its duties.

'Alliances' with corporations, or what wishful thinking describes as coalitions between members of the civil society, does not, however, meet with universal approval. The corporations' involvement is part and parcel of their marketing and branding, their priority is to align their philanthropic policy with their business needs, and often their charitable donations are not supported by a Socially Responsible Investment policy. Bill Gates, in this instance, is accused of investing his endowments in companies which cause the poverty and disease his foundation has committed to help eradicate. While the corporations' commitment to good causes amounts to something which is much less than it looks as corporate funding in the US and the UK is only 3 - 5 per cent of total giving, this commitment is also sometimes questionable: philanthropic funds established by business barons are suspected of being there in order primarily to shield their benefactors from payments to the government rather than help others.

Corporations with enough power to force even governments to capitulate, may be willing to enter into 'alliances' with celebrities or NGOs in order to address public concerns regarding their role, restore public trust in their business and gain credibility. But at the same time they make sure that they always maintain the upper hand in this relationship, use their connections for PR purposes, and take the NGOs expertise to conduct more profitable business in the low-rent neighbourhoods of the world.

It follows that the more 'civilised' and domesticated the NGOs become, the more their capacity to instigate change is diluted. Hence, and as opposed to Greenpeace which is committed to working with corporations, Christian Aid, a Church-backed agency, distrusting big business, avoids 'alliances' of this kind. As its representative put it, 'we do not want to do anything that is going to limit our ability to be critical'. It looks as if in the future the dividing line between aid agencies will be drawn between those who take the corporations' money and those who refuse to.

The tactics of the NGOs have accordingly been readjusted. Their campaigning shifted away from traditional forms of protest – petitions, pickets or mass demonstrations. What they use, instead, is briefings, press stories, lobbying, emailing, legal and also occasionally direct action, which is sometimes pregnant with unintentional developments. The Internet is both a channel for communication and a mass organiser. In the case of the 'hacktivists', it also turns into the means of attack on the websites of the corporate world, including that of the World Trade Organisation. Campaigns are based on research rather than claims, and are often run by individuals who have worked for government, international agencies or corporations.

In spite of their relentless fight for members, money and media attention, in spite also of their unaccountability, the inevitable bureaucratisation, and accusations that they pursue single issues at the expense of the broader good, NGOs ability to influence legislation, regulation and international treaties is growing. But even if, as the German system theorist Niklas Luhmann has argued, the sphere of communication becomes more and more differentiated, specialised, institutionalised and professionalised, or if, as Cornel West, the Afro-American Harvard University professor, has put it, 'gallant efforts to reconstruct public-mindedness in a balkanised society of proliferating identities and constituencies seem far-fetched, if not futile', NGOs can still open up a very important dialogue which can possibly revitalise the public sphere. The scrutiny to which they subject the policy of various government departments offers a learning experience in the form of moral insights, knowledge prohibited to the layman, and communicative action. It also creates new possibilities for the structural development of capitalist democracy. Evolution, as Jürgen Habermas held, means 'the realisation of an ordered sequence of structural possibilities'.

The NGOs role as relief agencies is more controversial. Relying often on governments which rely on them to give their policies the moral authority and the legitimacy that has gone missing, they appear to be implementing policies decided by national governments. Their work is politicised, indeed, used by governments when they are keen to prove, as the Americans do, that 'American generosity' equals 'American values in action' or, more importantly, when aid donors, rather than help nations to help their own people, seek to dictate how and where supplies are to be distributed. This is nothing less than philanthropic imperialism.

The credibility of the NGOs is, further, fatally compromised when they are perceived as no more than offshoots of the West's military activities, Neo-Governmental Organisations acting as the unofficial representatives of a bankrupt policy, agents of the West. This is what happened in Kosovo where, while Anglo-American forces bombed Belgrade, the supposedly neutral aid workers were working with allied troops at the frontier with Macedonia. The story is the same in Rwanda, Somalia, Afghanistan and Iraq where relief agencies, so identified with the West, were seen by the local communities as part and parcel of the West's involvement in the regions.

As Western policy on aid has no long-term objectives and as aid to the poor is becoming an industry, the NGOs are becoming increasingly important. To meet the requirements of their mission, they need, however, to resist the inevitable bureaucratisation, likely to turn them into institutions as rigid as the state and as self-seeking as the corporations. They need further to adhere strictly to their commitments in line with their code of conduct which states explicitly that they are 'not to act as instruments of government foreign policy'. This is as vital for their existence as is transparency and accountability to their members and the public, the standards of which need to be substantially improved. Good standards include transparent bookkeeping, regular assessments and ethical fundraising.

As important is, likewise, the objective assessment of their contribution to the causes they are committed to support. Both the donors, who contribute billions of dollars, and the state, which offers the NGOs tax subsidies, need to know what benefits their contribution has produced. Donors and taxpayers cannot subsidise the airlifting of bottled water from Britain to Sri Lanka at an estimated cost of about $4 a kilo. But this, I am sure, is like preaching virtue to the cardinals.

However, the problem is not solved even if all the above conditions are met, for the democratic deficit remains. Power cannot be handed over to pressure groups even if the latter have won an iconic status. Groups deal only with a small portion of quantifiable concerns that make sense in the context of the institutions, and they are useful insofar as they try, sometimes with some success, to correct imbalances in a disequilibrated world. But they cannot defeat the system of meanings and values of a demeaned structure just as they cannot make the summer wait for them to finish a report on climate change. Donor or cream democracy is not an option. Such democracy takes us back to corporatist social models which give control of important areas of social or economic life to an unelected élite to the exclusion of the citizenry. The only option is citizens' democracy. Unimaginable under current circumstances, this option will nevertheless always be there like tomorrow's sky.

5. Good, But Not Good Enough

Unable to influence governments whose diminished role is a cause of the most serious concern, even despairing of them, citizens, as consumers this time, have turned to the corporations expecting them to do what governments fail to. Corporations, though seen by the public as rapacious and socially irresponsible, are supposed to listen to their customers' demands because consumer power, towards which the vendors of goods or policies have the utmost respect, determines the product itself; and the product-range had better be as diverse as possible. The saints factory of Pope John Paul II produced a new saint in the person of Josemaria Escriva, the Founder of the Spanish and most reactionary *Opus Dei* movement, but, in order to satisfy a different kind of customer, it also beatified Jewish-born Edith Stein, a Catholic nun killed in the gas chambers.

Expectations were built on the assumption that citizens as consumers can somehow force the corporations which walk out of step with our time to honour their social, ethical and environmental responsibilities. Voting with their cash, it was assumed, citizens can help to bring business under some form of public control, curb their power and thereby turn the world into a more civilised place in which to live. The same belief, incidentally, created the illusion that in our world elitism and hierarchy have been eroded.

The ensuing shift in expectations has, indeed, put the corporations under increasing pressure. They need to prove to a sceptical public, which continues to distrust the oligopolies, that as good corporate citizens, they not only act within the law but they also respect the rights of the rightless, enhance social wellbeing and care about the environment. Social accountability, social auditing, social investment, good corporate governance and proper business ethics have won in the last decade the respectability considered to be necessary if businesses are to maintain the confidence of their customers. Failure to prove their virtuous intentions can make their reputation look like a blasted tree, lose them markets and hit their share price. Conversely, an ethical policy can strengthen a company's market position and increase returns.

Although being, or rather looking virtuous costs money, corporations do, thus, respond to pressure. The response is not overwhelming, but it is there. Nestlé and Cadbury, accused of turning a blind eye to child slavery in the cocoa industry, cannot carry on as before, and pharmaceuticals, led by GlaxoSmithKline and Merck, had no choice but to abandon their lawsuit in South Africa to protect their patents on anti-Aids drugs. Financial Goliaths – Barclays, Citigroup, Merrill Lynch, Credit Suisse and others – were forced by animal rights protesters to withdraw the financial services they provided to a UK animal testing company; and although Tony Blair sided with Monsanto, the big supermarket chains rather than face the inevitable consumer unrest banned GM foods from their shelves. Shell, stung by attacks on its activities in Nigeria, first denounced by Ken Saro-Wiwa, the first martyr of the contemporary anti-capitalist movement who was hanged by the Nigerian authorities in Port Harcourt in November 1995, and by the Brent Spa disposal, was likewise forced to acknowledge its wider responsibilities. Even McDonald's, out of its depth, requested its egg suppliers to give their hens more space.

The change, which in any case amounts to very much less than it appears in reports, has been brought about by pressure, not only from without, but also from within. Big shareholders have often been ready to challenge the corporate culture's unethical, even illegal, practices ranging from the release of misleading information to corruption, and from unethical investment policies to outright fraud. Institutional investors have even begun to demand, apart from a decent return on their investment, socially and environmentally responsible choices. Some have warned companies that they can no longer ignore shifting public opinion on social responsibility.

Yet, socially responsible investment, which is not all that easy to define precisely, comprises only a tiny proportion of global investment, and 'rich-nation moral priorities', with which the NGOs 'load' governments and corporations, has only a minimum impact. At the same time, those who say we have already made too many commitments to decency are not missing. The grounds on which opposition to commitments grows is fear that developing nations, immune to NGO pressures, will find in them new market opportunities, which, when grabbed, will turn Shanghai, Singapore and the United Arab Emirates into alternatives to London and New York.

Good as far as it goes, consumer and shareholder power does not, however, go far enough. Ethics, in the first place, contain an element of uncertainty. Using underpaid Third-World children to stitch footballs is wrong but letting them starve without any work is also wrong. Doing, on the other hand, the right thing in one area does not give the corporation a certificate of innocence. United Fruit, the first truly multinational corporation, assuming its 'corporate social responsibility', supplied earthquake relief to help Nicaragua in 1972, while its head, Sam 'the Banana Man' Zemurray donated part of his fortune to a children's clinic in New Orleans and later $1m to the city's university to finance 'Middle American' research. But

United Fruit, as Peter Chapman said in his disturbingly informative *Jungle Capitalists: A Story of Globalisation*, in the quest for its unhallowed grail, also financed many 'regime changes' in Central America, including the coup that overthrew the government of Guatemala in 1954, and the failed Bay of Pigs invasion in 1961 to overthrow Cuba's Fidel Castro. Likewise, Barclays tells us how many personal computers it junked, but not how much money it has lent to the world's arms manufacturers. Nor did Tesco bother to explain how many small shopkeepers its expansion programme put out of business.

Consumer power has serious limitations. Consumer and shareholder power does not challenge the free market ideology and its bloodless *coup d'état*, nor did it prevent the Force 12 Enron scandal and the collapse of other corporations amid the most serious allegations of corruption, deceit, greed and incompetence, to which capitalism still remains very loyal. It is also fundamentally flawed. It sanctions the running of the system by an extremely wealthy minority, which, being unelected and unaccountable, cannot be displaced except through a successful global anti-capitalist uprising as easy to accomplish as draining the sea. With power handed over to corporations, democracy can count itself among the dead, a shadow and a recollection. Miserably, democracy is moving toward the ultimate frontiers of darkness even if consumer and shareholder power could match the power of the multinationals, for the system would be empowering, not everybody, but only the converts to the free market economy and the affluent middle class. The poor and those who object to a society run by the market would be left out in the cold.

In accepting the status quo, consumer democracy has also to accept all its consequences. By subscribing tacitly to the values and culture of the market's globalism, it endorses the commercialisation of all aspects of life and of all sectors, including science, education and culture, which are all forced to abandon their purpose and measure their achievements in terms dictated by the market – what sells. It has also to accept the colonization of the world, the fact that whole countries, from the Third to the First World, are forced to dance to the tunes of the IMF, the WTO or the World Bank, to open their markets to the moneyed conglomerates of the West, to deregulate, privatise, de-unionise, reduce the state's involvement in the welfare of their people, give up their fair trade rights, and make painful economic concessions to corporations to attract or maintain their investment.

Despite its verisimilitude, the same consumer democracy is responsible for the plundering of tribal cultures, the commercialisation of their traditions, the consumption of their past by the West, all of it in the name, in this case, of appreciation and love. Rather than diminish, the gruesome global inequality and injustice is, thus, perpetuated and, indeed, reinforced.

Nothing, of course, is unusual about it all. Corporations have not been created to save the planet, and they will, therefore, never battle for justice, equality or freedom. Concerns of such a nature are none of their business. They cannot, therefore, be expected, as playwright Jean Giraudoux might have said, to dispatch a plane to Java for a bouquet of flowers or a steamer to Egypt for a basket of figs as a present to the public. They are not the guardians of the public interest, and no consumer and shareholder power can force them to play such a role. Besides, they should never be the guardians. No such authority has ever been conferred upon them, and, one can hope, it never will be.

Citizens do not need protection. 'I would, yes, I would rather see the Greeks wander round the world with outstretched arms, begging for bread, than have protectors', Andreas Kalvos penned angrily in the nineteenth century when the Powers of the time determined right and wrong on the strength of their own interests. This, in turn, means that consumers should never aspire to become social regulators. This is the citizens' job.

Working on it is not, however, as easy as working on our tan.

6. Beyond the Price of Sausages

Globalism, just like iron, whose discovery led to the manufacture of new weapons, or electricity which may be used occasionally by torturers to extract information from their victims, is not a threat. The threat is represented, instead, by the people behind it, the forces which, motivated by arrogance and greed, are determined to conquer, dominate and destroy what stands in their way.

The rich clubs of the English football Premier League, owned by billionaires, have the right under the free market system and open competition to buy as many overseas players as they like, i.e., the right to buy success rather than nurture it organically at home. But by doing so, they undermine the integrity of sport, leave unattended its grassroots development once nurtured by the local community, and erode the quality of the English national team. Further, by paying salaries as high as £100,000 a week, in other words, money good enough to attract top mercenaries, they raise the cost of their ventures, which nevertheless the supporters are happy to meet because all they care about is their club's success even if it has not been won but bought.

This development is bad not just for football. It is also bad for civil society, which it corrupts, because, instead of standing up and being counted, the latter allows itself to be bought off by big money. Incidentally, Uefa and Fifa, the football's European and world governing bodies respectively, try to modify the system, but for the rich clubs, those whose inflexible omnipresence is very different from their winsome photo, the suggested modifications are 'heavy-handed and unworkable'.

Corruption of the civil society through fake grassroots campaigns by public relations professionals in the pay of large corporations is not an unusual phenomenon, potentially involving anyone heavily dependent on corporate funds. Corporations do not spend the extraordinary amounts of money they do on public relations for nothing – and bribes accepted, Demosthenes, the Athenian fourth century BC statesman warned his compatriots, vanquish the taker. Edward Bernays, the 'father of public relations' who brought the discipline of his uncle, Sigmund Freud, to the marketplace, explained their rationale in his seminal 1928 book, *Propaganda*. Being society's 'intelligent minority', he said, corporations have a 'duty' to manipulate the unthinking public for the sake, of course, of freedom and democracy. Power corrupts but, as it happens, weakness does not support virtue, either. As a result nothing changes without the conglomerates' assent or at least without the refinements which would make any proposed changes acceptable to their board.

The challenge posed by the corporations' global order and all its underlying assumptions is gigantic, beyond the scope anything existing resistance networks can do to meet. Although those with Ph.Ds in quietness will never acknowledge it, power is having its sway. Rather than humanised, globalisation as understood by the hoggish market forces and liberal imperialism, is getting more aggressive, more centrally controlled, more resistant to civilising influences, more rapacious than ever. This is the case particularly as the new and powerful global forces which have emerged in the Third World, in China, India, Russia, Brazil or the Gulf states, immune to any pressure exerted by Western ethical networks, are happy to do nothing more than volunteer disdainful looks at anything not designed to increase their wealth.

It follows that to be effective, the civil society's institutions need to be strengthened, i.e., enabled to function without the existing financial restraints. But this can be done only if the state steps in to subsidise them. I very much doubt, however, whether this is what David Cameron, the British Conservative party leader, had in mind when he said that the focus of his party will shift away from the traditional tax and spending issues because now, in 'the post-Marxist age', politics is 'all about our society and the relations of government to it'.

Meanwhile, Western NGOs, concerned only with aspects of the

whole, cannot even embrace a vision of a different world because such a world is beyond their horizons or, more precisely, their terms of reference. Hence, in the first place, the need for a constructive vision of the global future, the vision of a world as respectful of the environment and human rights as of different cultures and civilisations. This is the oecumenical vision – 'songs', to recall Horace, 'never heard before' – which values life as opposed to the globalist vision of a world which values profits. Far from perfection, but close to heart, it is the voice of Justice in the moving chaos of our time.

Economic growth, a God to be worshipped, is not an end in itself and cannot be unlimited. As the Greeks demonsrated, progress, likewise, is not identical to profit maximisation. Besides, the entire globe, though thanks to satellite television can delight in the Eurovision Song contest, can never really enjoy the living standards of the First World. The planet will not support 12bn or even 8bn people living the way the North lives now. The strain is already intolerable, and the earth actually is almost ready to force upon us a post-material growth. Yet, though capitalist growth is no longer sustainable, the North's model has become the universal model of development, which is why people such as Indian writer Ramachandra Guha view calls to the Third World by 'green missionaries' to lower its expectations as another attempt to dispossess further the world's poor and indigenous people.

The North can hardly set the tone of the discussion unless it accepts that sustainability does not begin at the Third World whose basic infrastructural needs plus those for education, health care and energy must be met. Like charity, it begins at home with all of us changing our way of life, our aspirations and above all our appetites. To survive, we need much more than 'Save the Planet' concerts and awesome shows of environmentally friendly ass and belly dances. We need, instead, a revolution which will give flesh to the Socratic axiom never in want, the parent of meanness and viciousness, and never in wealth, the parent of indolence. Turning wealth into the goal of one's life is, as Freud said, a pathological symptom, a feature of a neurotic, mentally unbalanced person. Thoughtless consumption is, on the other hand, a symptom of the insanity to which the individual is driven by a culture which has identified progress with the ludicrous belief that more is always better. No 'Save the Planet' campaign can ever expect to succeed if the greed of both the multinationals and the globalised individual is not confined to the cellars of our existence, if we do not re-establish the connections that give communities the sense of common purpose, and if we do not look for personal fulfilment outside the market context and its indices.

Whatever the world's leading military powers might be prepared to do to sustain it, equally unsustainable in the long run is also the Anglo-American new world order. A world in which the top 20 per cent of the population receives 83 per cent of its wealth, while the bottom 20 per cent gets less than 1.5 per cent of it is hardly likely to be a peaceful world. Greed and peace are incompatible.

Globalisation has never promised free drinks or pizzas. Even so, it can be acceptable provided it benefits us all, not just the US, so far its main beneficiary, and the élites of the West. It has to protect the environment against 'progress' – the kind of progress that came with smallpox, brought unwittingly to the New World by Columbus, that weakened and demoralised the Inca Empire – and use the world's natural resources sparingly and for the benefit of all, including future generations. It has to provide security of existence to everyone and everything under the sun. Cultures and languages, asphyxiating under the pressure of American pop culture's homogenisation drive, need to be able to breathe again, communities need to be protected and democracy, whose springs of existence seem to give way, has to be given the means to resist the erosion of its foundations. Nations, likewise, need to feel secure against hegemonism, American or otherwise. Fundamentally, the rights of everyone and everything need to be protected against the onslaught of the forces of capitalism if globalisation is to be a move forward to a future holding promises rather than threats.

All this necessitates the reinstatement of Justice as the supreme principle to which everything is subordinated. Justice in its Greek sense is the force which will come to the rescue of the wretched and destitute and eradicate the current horrible inequalities between and within nations the like of which the world has never seen before. It will ensure that people live freely in their own land, secure, without anxiety and fear of the future, masters of their fate and of their natural resources, honoured for who they are. Justice will protect their traditions, culture and language, and will treat nature with all respect due to her. As a distributive force, Justice will not, and cannot, offer every member of the human race Louis Vuitton leather bags and Tiffany jewels. It can, however, give them the basics, including dignity without which people cannot live.

To protect a nation against moneyed forces bigger than itself, stop the economy falling prey to forces of unrestrained greed, restore the integrity of the political system, shelter the civil society and protect the rights of the individual, the powers of the huge corporations need to be curtailed. Oligopolies, the forces that corner the market by buying a dominant and controlling long position, are anathema even to the free market itself. Adam Smith, the intellectual father of free market economics, made it clear in his condemnation of monopoly power back in 1776. These oligopolies, commanding total and unrestrained power, need to be broken in the free market's own name. Split into smaller units, the world's largest corporations – the General Motors, Wal-Marts and Exxon Mobils of this world – will be less able to dictate their policies to governments and even to the market itself, and hold the world to ransom. Concentration of power has really gone so far that even the world's accounting industry is dominated by just four firms through their global accounting networks (KPMG, Deloitte, PwC and Ernst & Young) which control 69 per cent of global accounting fees. The European Union needs to break them up at least to preserve, if nothing else, competition itself.

Even if one is to accept the argument advanced by corporations such as Wal-Mart that its buying power is in the interests of the consumers as much as the power of trade unions is in the interests of the workers, the almost dictatorial power Wal-Mart has assumed over central functions of the US economy makes it, not only an uninvited, but also an unwelcome defender of consumer interests. Progress, in any case, is not measured by the cents the consumer saves when buying his or her sausages. If it was, Stalinist Russia ought to be the model. The price of sausages cannot dictate the level of our freedoms.

To protect the latter, the state's intervention through regulation is indispensable, for the state is not there to guard the interests of the multinationals and make possible the creation of what former French prime minister Lionel Jospin called a 'market society'.

7. The Market or the Citizens

The role of the state was questioned by British prime minister Margaret Thatcher and US president Ronald Reagan back in the '80s when they launched their assault to 'push back the boundaries of the state'. The boundaries were, indeed, pushed back in their countries, and the free market was given a free hand that led to the erosion of state power. Anything but fixed, these boundaries are, however, constantly rocking back and forth like a Hassidat before the Wailing Wall in order to meet societies' increasing or decreasing expectations. The corporations, obviously, will fight tooth and nail to keep the state out of their way – the only role of the state, a minimal state, for the libertarian tradition of Harvard philosophy professor Robert Nozick is the role of the nightwatchman. This increasingly becomes the case as the dominant position the new financial capitalism has achieved in the last twenty-five years has ensured the marginalisation of both national capital and the national state. The paradox is that its hold over the state has increased at a time that decentralisation is in some instances on the increase and ownership of the state has somehow spread.

Focusing on the latter, Robert Dahl, 'the Dean' of American political scientists, holds that the modern state is a polyarchy, i.e. a structure containing multiple centres of power that work in contention, but also in cooperation, with each other. For the pluralist view, which admittedly looks a much more attractive option for bedtime reading than the telephone directory, there is no state bias in favour of the corporative world. There is no set of institutionally-based elites, i.e. leaders of big organisations – corporate, nonprofit or governmental, either, which according to another theory, the elite theory, inevitably dominate all large-scale societies. Policies are formed as a result of pressures applied by a variety of organised interests, including environmental, consumer and civil rights groups none of which can nevertheless claim success in passing legislation againt the opposition of the corporations.

Others, the institutionalists, assert state policy is fundamentally moulded by the institutions in which it is embedded. One of them, Theda Skocpol, suggests that the state functionaries, having interests of their own which they pursue independently, or in conflict with society can to an important degree formulate policy autonomously. Yet for others, the state is controlled by individuals, who, making strategic choices along the lines of the game theory according to which players make decisions in an attempt to maximise their profits, create the conditions for the estabishment of a hegemonic system that suits the needs of the winners.

But class-inspired theories can hardly be overlooked. The function of the state, Nicos Poulantzas, the Greek political sociologist who died tragically in 1979, aged 43, held, benefits the capitalist class. But, as he insisted, the state is 'relatively autonomous'. Politicians try to advance the interests of capitalism through rules embodied in the state's very institutional form, but their prime concern is stability and material expansion. They do also have to attend to the concerns of the civil society, from the media and trade unions to the Church and NGOs, what Jürgen Habermas called the public sphere, which is autonomous from the state and yet part of it. Keeping the latter happy is not too difficult when it comes to issues relating to issues such as gay rights. But the desire to please ends where the interests of people like Rupert Murdoch – the man with a direct telephone line to prime minister Blair – are affected. It appears that, though integrated into many sections of the civil society, the state, at least in the Anglo-Saxon world, has abandoned even the pretence of neutrality in what in effect is a war between society and the corporations – the banks, the energy industry, the drug companies among others.

An ethical society cannot, however, exist without sufficient checks and balances as the Athenian democracy has shown. Unlimited economic power exploits the providers of goods and services but also the consumers, corrupts the political system and also society, and distorts the priorities of the nation. Anti-corruption laws are futile if the conglomerates and their policies corrupt public opinion and poison it with their ruthless values, the unprincipled, crude pursuit of selfish interests. Democracy has, indeed, no future if it fails to provide the guarantees a free society needs, solid safety nets for those whom globalisation is letting down, safe core public services such as education and healthcare for everybody, the fair distribution of the wealth generated by everybody's work, the fees we pay to living, and a media free from the tutelage of media barons. To be acceptable, globalisation has to provide more guarantees: to communities, cultures, languages, the future and the past. Leaving matters to the free market is an act of faith, and faith in a decent free market future comes in very short supply.

The state has all the power, and often exercises it, to maintain some desired standards. The British Advertising Standards Authority responds to complaints made by the public and forces companies to withdraw offensive advertisements, UK water companies can be forced to stop water leaks which result in water shortages, employers have been forced to adopt a policy of positive discrimination, smokers have been banned from all enclosed public spaces and companies are encouraged through incentives to develop alternative sources of energy. The state can in the future, if it so desires, even subsidise plastic surgery to turn the British into the best-looking Europeans. There are no limits to what the government can do, and this includes spreading the benefits of living in the modern world more widely.

However, the power of the state has been ruthlessly used in the past twenty-five years only to privatise virtue and nationalise vice – hand over national assets to corporations, cut public spending and regulation, liberalise the labour market, cut the power of the Unions, decrease tax for the wealthy and give a free reign to the free market's voracious forces. The power is there but the governments committed to the free market will not use it against the big players to lift billions of people out of poverty and reduce or even just stop the rising inequalities. Yet, this power, which not too long ago was viewed by radicals as the enemy of the working class, has to be used. The current gross inequalities are obscene and corporations, getting bigger than the state itself, threaten its power which in a democracy is or should be the power of the citizens. The dictatorship of the market is only round the corner.

The argument in favour of far greater state involvement in the business of the money machine, which in the last decade has, as a financial writer commented, mutated into 'a vast, shadowy, multi-headed hydra', is far greater than ever before because, not just the public, but even the legislators themselves do not understand how the ultra-complex financial instruments work. The new capitalism is inaccessible even to the well-educated classes – people see staggering wealth amassed by a few without a clue as to who has paid for it.

In any case, efficient use of resources, which is the argument in favour of 'modernisation', is not the only criterion on the strength of which policy should be made. Even if efficiently produced, take-away food is still take-away food. As important is the spirit in which services are rendered, the goals of the activities undertaken, the civic ethos cultivated. Progress, if this is the reason individuals engage in various ventures, is not measured in monetary terms, which is what businesses do. It is measured, instead, in terms of human happiness which in turn is assessed by the individual's fulfilment in his or her personal, professional and social life, his or her doing something that is socially and ethically validated, the sense of purpose in one's life in a world the individual feels he or she belongs rather than is alienated from. Progress is not turning the individual into a money-making machine in the service of faceless shareholders.

Even if privately-owned business entities can financially perform better than publicly-owned ones, the latter and not the former need to run the schools and the universities, the hospitals and the social services, anything that provides a service to the public. Determined to maintain their academic standards, Oxford and Cambridge universities have in this sense made clear that they do not want control of their governing bodies by an external board representing the business world.

The state needs also to be present in the defence of core sectors of the economy against foreign takeovers and corporate raiders committed to nothing but profit. Undistorted market competition may be good for the multinationals and, in theory, even the consumer, but it is the enemy of everything else that stands outside the flow of money. Protectionism is, of course, anathema to the free marketeers. Whatever the latter think, citizens need, however, to keep control of their destiny, communities to retain their identity and nations to safeguard their future. Strategic sectors of the economy cannot be handed over to unreliable multinational economic forces or state-controlled foreign funds as much as the defence of the country cannot be outsourced to a foreign Power. Were they to be handed over, the community would be at the mercy of corporations and private equity firms some of which are not averse to the pursuit of political ends;

it would have, in effect, surrendered its future to the nondescript, greedy world of the multinationals. The age of innocence is in any case already well behind as the June 2007 EU summit decided to drop references to 'undistorted competition'.

The movement against foreign takeovers is gaining momentum on both sides of the Atlantic as both national states feel threatened by the increasing power of Chinese, Russian and Middle Eastern funds, and communities worry about their future. Hillary Clinton, the US leading presidential candidate, articulated this fear quite brutally when she rejected a trade deal with South Korea. Such a deal, she said in a way that demonstrated the limits of globalisation, would 'hurt the US car industry, increase our trade deficit, cost us middle-class jobs and make America less competitive'. The US remains, of course, fully committed to its rejection of protectionism when the latter is practised by other countries.

Further, and as necessity is the mother of invention, to cut the corporations' influence the state needs to restrict their size and capitalisation, and ban mergers and acquisitions if the new entity is to control more than a certain section of each sector. It can also force the multinationals to break into smaller units, which is what the EU is trying to achieve, for example, in the case of Europe's big electricity and natural gas companies. Of course, corporations, like all free enterprise enthusiasts, hate competition in any form as British Airways and other airlines were only too eager to prove. Hence stripping the energy companies of their networks provides no guarantee that they will not build cartels, which, again the EU is determined to prevent. It will not stop them, either, from keeping prices too high as the UK's energy suppliers have been doing. The benefits to the consumer of the free market's price war have not exactly been delivered. Beneficiaries are the corporations. Aggressive enforcement of anti-trust and anti-cartel policies is, thus, the only solution if the immense power of the oligopolies is to be rolled back. But such a policy requires statesmanship, and the latter, as Demosthenes said, requires moral courage.

The state can further control through taxes the corporations' profits, or, alternatively, set a legal profit cap beyond which all money made is returned to the consumers in the form of price reductions. The excessive and ethically unjustified remuneration of top executives has also to be curbed, and 'golden parachutes' to company bosses banned altogether. Nobody, absolutely nobody, needs to earn that much money – 'stupid money'. Such measures are bound, of course, to be welcomed by the corporations as much as turkeys welcome the arrival of Christmas – to escape them, they will look for tax heavens offered by rogue states of a different complexion to those that figured in US president Bush's cosmic masterplan. Greek shipowners have made the point forcefully enough for the Greek state to take notice. The problem can be solved, but not if a country acts on her own because no country on her own can find the solution.

The state can also demand before action is taken the consent of all those affected by the corporation's activities, including its workforce, the local communities and environmental groups, and prohibit donations or 'loans', often undisclosed, to political parties. Such donations distort the nature of democracy as corporations and private funds will support only those prepared to act in their favour or, at least, those who will never object to their activities. The European Union can be of help here by introducing relevant legislation as it can also introduce class action lawsuits, which can give consumers the right of collective redress against corporations and their bankers, lawyers and accountants who rip them off or who provide defective goods or services. The corporations' argument that such a measure would reduce their global competitiveness is hollow. Bad practice cannot be protected whatever the reason.

The need for state intervention is far greater when it comes to media ownership, which highly concentrated, and also, ironically, the least transparent and accountable of all, threatens competition, endangers public service broadcasting and raises public interest concerns. The media, whose 'first freedom', Marx so pointedly said, 'consists in its not being a business', would have to be subject to the strictest possible checks and controls. Oligopolies in the increasingly deregulated multimedia world offer no guarantee of fairness or balance in the presentation of news. For the Rupert Murdochs, Silvio Berlusconis and Conrad Blacks information is just another commodity. The media empires need to be broken, and media barons should own no more than one newspaper and one TV station. The dismantling of their empires is the very first step on the long road towards citizen emancipation, achieved once and then lost in the suburbs of consumerism.

Gigantism is incompatible with the spirit of democracy whether we are talking about media empires, corporations or states. Though hiding behind economic necessities, gigantism in economic life is the apotheosis of greed in terms of everything: money, power, status, all that is considered to be the crown of a life of success. But it is exactly this excessive economic power, which is bound to be abused, that requires its drastic reduction. Gigantism and democracy, indeed gigantism and life, are mutually exclusive.

The same is true in the case of national states, too. Small is better as a matter of principle or, at least, this is what the Greeks thought out of conviction rather than necessity. The proper limits of the state, Plato held, can increase or decrease, but, whatever the case, they have to be consistent with the unity of purpose that expresses the aspirations of its citizens. Without it, a state is nothing more than a supermarket. One cannot, of course, expect state entities to break into their constituent parts in eager anticipation of a new, democratic world order. But split amicably into small and yet viable units as in Czechoslovakia, nation states would be unable to dominate the world just as ethnic majorities would be unable to dominate ethnic minorities if the latter could establish their own national units. Small entities would also make the citizens' personal involvement in their running more likely. This will not lead, as the neoliberals foresee, to the demise of the state, a unit, they believe, is bound to go like the traditional city, the child of the nineteenth century. But the state will be radically transformed.

Encouraging the break up of large national entities such as the US, Russia or China, may, of course, have other implications which cannot be disregarded. But the diminution of the large states' power through devolution is of cardinal importance if the gap between the all too powerful entities and the rest of the world is to be bridged and democracy, international in this instance, is to have some bodily substance.

Devolution, of course, is not good by definition. It is, indeed, meaningless if small entities with a pugilistic reputation such as those in the Balkans, rather than make the best of what they have won, throw themselves with much ardour into vicious ethnic wars which brutalise society even further and kill the moral instinct. Nor does smallness offer a guarantee of economic stability, social justice, public order or democracy; and, rather than eliminate, it could even reinforce the current worldwide unequalising trends as prosperous areas could well cut the poor ones out. It will not, at any rate, close by itself the gaps between the European Union and the US, the developing world and the developed countries, the technology-based economies and the agricultural ones, the capital-importing and capital-exporting countries; and there is no reason why small state units should not carry on the European Union's agricultural protectionism, the US's import restrictions, or the rich countries' building up of their exports through subsidies.

Small is beautiful but only in the right circumstances, if, in other words, institutional change is accompanied by change at the cultural and the personal level, transforming the whole way of thinking and living of our time. Structural changes, often encumbered with excess luggage, are meaningless without cultivation of public virtue, and the latter cannot be sustained, as the Greeks believed, without a personal commitment to it.

Yet some steps towards a new international architecture, a new democratic world order founded on a Justice that respects natural limits and opposes excesses can possibly be taken. The key factor here is the revitalisation of the UN, the most important international institution that is nevertheless stuck in the mid-twentieth century. A new global coalition under the auspices of the United Nations, both its General Assembly and the various Agencies, may well be established and granted all the power it needs to act in the interests of the entire world. This is already happening to some extent as all member states have accepted responsibility to protect people threatened by genocide and comparable crimes, and have contributed towards an improved emergency relief fund, a democracy fund, an ethics office and a tougher system for protecting whistleblowers.

But the UN should certainly get more ambitious, and get, in the first place, actively involved in all efforts to stop global warming. The EU has taken the lead in this respect by setting its most ambitious environmental targets – the cutting of carbon emissions by 20 per cent between 1990 and 2020. This is partly to be achieved through the development of renewable energy, which is expensive, and hence about a dozen countries, mostly Eastern European, relying heavily on traditional forms of energy, are not eager to adopt this target, at least in the short-term. Costs come into the picture in Western Europe as well as business groups have indicated that, if cornered, energy-intensive companies would relocate outside Europe, in India, China or other countries which may well decide to carry on using cheaper fossil fuels with impunity. Any measures need, therefore, to take into account international competition, which is what makes imperative the conclusion of a global agreement on greenhouse gas emissions in the context of the UN.

Incidentally, to reduce the size of the carbon footprint many more, and drastic, measures may well need to be introduced in a way that can end globalisation as we know it. They can affect everything, from food, which writer Barbara Kingsolver estimated reaches the average American household after having travelled 1,500 miles, to global trade and travel. They can disrupt both the existing world economic order and the lifestyle of the West far beyond anything currently imagined. Miserably, they can also set communities, nations and even continents against each other in what has already been given a name – ecowars.

Special UN Agencies can further implement policies decided by the General Assembly to combat killer-diseases, illiteracy, and water, food and energy shortages. The millennium development goal to reduce poverty by 2015, which will be missed by a mile, is another story that needs to be given priority. Special law-enforcement UN Agencies can conduct the worldwide battle against drugs, crime, slavery, forced or bonded labour, torture, money laundering, human cloning or the denial of trade union rights. Special UN conferences can further be held to legislate on a number of issues such as bringing the distribution of small arms under control. In theory at least, the possibility of action is there as shown by the UN Global Compact ethical business initiative taken to 'work against corruption in all its forms, including extortion and bribery'. The problem is, of course, that the 'business community' opposes the legal enforcement of corporate obligations, which in any case cannot be enforced as the UN lacks the relevant resources.

An UN coalition can legitimately 'declare war' for the protection of human rights and the world's cultural heritage. It can coordinate a fairer distribution of the world's wealth and the provision of better health and education in the poorest countries. It can also ensure the removal of the nuclear threat which makes even the distant stars shiver, force the dislodgement of unelected transnational rulers of the world and prevent civil wars and ethnic cleansing. To 'smoke' its enemies 'out', the UN coalition will need all the powers a government has, legislative, executive and judicial; and to win these powers it will have to overcome the inevitable opposition of the major world players, the US in particular. In order not to end up replacing the national state's bureaucracy with another bureaucracy, international this time, NGOs will also have to be more actively involved in the work of the UN Agencies. Currently, 3,000 of them, including many without the right qualifications, have consultative status.

The problem is that any UN reform is fiercely contested between the rich and powerful Western Powers, which place the emphasis on security, and the developing world which would like to see policies that lead to a fairer global economic order. Security as an issue is quite controversial as what is terrorism for the one side is resistance to illegal occupation for the other. There are also difficulties regarding the distribution of power within the organisation as moving control from the General Assembly to the Secretariat is tantamount to handing over more power to the US, which would rather see no reform at all than permit the slightest dilution of her power.

This is, of course, the greatest of problems as the US in particular, but also other major Powers have reserved for themselves the right to determine future developments by intimidation or even raw military power. Such a policy was bound to fail even at the time US power had reached its peak, i.e. following the end of the cold war in 1989. It is even more likely to fail in today's conditions, when the international architecture is being redrawn and new challenges can be met only through cooperation between at least the leading powers.

Despite all difficulties, the UN is the international democratic forum where problems can be resolved, indeed, the only forum. The alternative is conflicts solved through the unbridled exercise of military power, which is bound to create new and far worse problems. A new world order can never be based on fear or unilateral dictation but on cooperation and respect for the rule of law. It cannot be achieved without self-accepted limits to the big players' power, the precondition of respect to which they are entitled. True in the past, this is still true today at a time when an expanding population, limited resources and rising materialist expectations are bound to stretch the world system to the breaking point.

But this is fiercely resisted by the Anglo-American 'liberal imperialism'. Heavily engaged in the 'war on terror', which provides the moral justification for the continuation of the war for vital resources, it refuses to engage in the war for Justice which would offer some relief to the 1.2bn people, those defined by the

World Bank as living without basic necessities and without hope, in conditions which have outgrown even fictional accounts of disaster. For human nature as nurtured by capitalism, enough is never enough because more is always better.

If disoriented, self-interest is a force more powerful than Reason or even hope.

8. Virtue and Guts

The market and its politicians have granted the people the freedom to choose their lifestyle, but they have not given them the responsibility for their choices or decision-making power – political, economic, technological or ecological. The right to choose is whisked away the moment the decision-making process is taken over by the market. But freedom does not exist without responsibility, which probably in current conditions most would do their best to avoid, and responsibility is meaningless without decision-making power. All three, freedom, responsibility and power to make decisions are at the core of both personal existence and citizenship, indispensable parts of the whole person, vital elements of a well-functioning democracy. They are also the yardstick by which the legitimacy of power can be measured. The assertion contains, however, nothing that, as I am well aware, would excite the curiosity of the pilgrims jostling for space in shopping malls, the temples of our culture.

The issue, political at its very core, is, therefore, the equal distribution of responsibility among the largest possible number of people, in effect, the shifting of power both within a national state and between states from the rich and powerful to everybody. Power, immune as it is to beneficial influences, has to spread horizontally and involve in its exercise all those affected by it along the lines of the Greek polis. Involvement of all people at grassroots level that enables citizens to develop human scale institutions is the most fundamental principle of an unchaperoned democracy.

The pivotal role which the citizens of the European Union can play in this respect can hardly be overstated. Their common political culture and repertoire of interpretive mechanisms and value systems can form the basis of a new global coalition towards the reconstruction of civil society as a citizens' society whose steering capacity can eventually force even the Union's own rigid institutions to reduce their democratic deficit. As Jürgen Habermas and Jacques Derrida stated the time mass demonstrations against the Iraq war had turned Europe into a zone of hope, a 'core Europe' has the ability to be the locomotive of a unifying project, and a new kind of politics, 'a transformative politics' that would connect with 'the motives and attitudes of the citizens themselves'. It is what can provide the testing ground for new democratic solutions to problems generated by the global challenges.

Europe has the ability and also needs to go further than that provided she can fill the current spiritual vacuum opened by, as German filmmaker Wim Wenders put it, the 'colonisation' of her soul by the Americans, find again the road to her destiny, and realise her potential. We must 'give Europe a soul', Angela Merkel, the German chancellor, likewise told her fellow European leaders. To some at least, this implies the liberation of Europe from American materialism and her re-connection with the values of her past, which can provide the alternative to the American dream. To some, such as the Hungarian primate Monsignor Peter Erdoe, this means a Christian Europe because 'without Christianity the heart of Europe would be missing'. To others, it means going back to what H.G. Wells called Greece's 'modern thinkers', those whose 'thoughts and creative and artistic impulse rose to levels that made their achievement a lamp to mankind for all the rest of history'. Going back to the roots will help us to rediscover our early spiritual commitment and reconnect with the humanistic ethos close to the European heart.

The European Union is, of course, confronted with practical

problems and disagreements over the essentials of the European project. With public opinion sceptical over, and apprehensive of, further initiatives following the latest wave of expansion, and with conflicting approaches to issues such as constitutional reforms, nuclear energy, foreign policy and common defence, or further expansion, the way ahead is full of challenges involving tedious compromises. Reaching the consensus between its 27 members that is needed to open the way to future developments is definitely a huge task, particularly as the US is only too happy to divide and rule when it suits her interests.

Still the EU has already reached a degree of integration unimaginable at the time it was established in 1957. It has provided the template for new forms of governance in the era of globalisation, including its body of laws, the celebrated *acquis communautaire*, and given the world the intellectual and moral leadership that can carry it to a democratic destination. If it decides at some point to stand up and be counted, its potential is enormous. Forcing the telecoms industry, and this despite the latter's fierce opposition, to slash its 'exorbitant roaming charges' by up to 70 per cent in 2007, was a landmark deal to this effect. It was, incidentally, denounced, by France Telecom as communist-style central planning.

The lead the EU has taken in further tackling global warming and energy security has placed it at the very front of the epic struggle for a safer world. This priority, together with other ones such as human rights, the social regulation of globalisation, the harmonisation of the corporate tax base across the union, peacekeeping, the reduction of poverty and a coherent foreign policy can only be handled by the Union as the embodiment of its members' collective will rather than by its individual member-states. So can a number of other issues ranging from security, immigration, energy, development trade and capital flows to working out a code of ethics for robot technology and combatting racism, across-border crime, xenophobia and terrorism.

The institutional structures and the principles on which these institutions rest, including cooperation rather than conflict, service rather than domination, tolerance rather than aggression, lawfulness rather than lawlessness, compromises rather than ultimatums, and, above all, freedom and democracy, provide all parties the safety they need to explore further their own democratic development. If globalisation has in the name of fairness to adopt the World Cup model, as former UN Secretary General Kofi Annan suggested, the European Union's model could equally well be England's Football Association. In such a case, the EU would be committed to making a just order 'accessible, enjoyable and safe for everyone regardless of race, religion, gender, sexuality, background or ability'. It would also be making itself responsible for establishing 'an efficient and fair regulatory structure' agreed by all its members that would ensure that this order is respected by all. Individual countries, just like the clubs, will still be able to maintain their independent course of action in an ethical environment.

The EU could not, and I would not like it, to become a superstate because the basic assumption here is that citizen participation in the affairs of the state is possible only in small entities. It is only then that people can share power and experiences, control their environment and connect their work, education, recreation, domestic living and private affairs to the common good. The time when the ethical was sought in the practices of small-scale communities, which since the days of social reformers Fourier and Owen have been seeking an alternative lifestyle to that provided by the market, has certainly gone. As a remnant of the past, the time when one's native town was thought of as the entire world, it is interesting but no more than the gallant expectation that a gentleman will refrain from smoking before ladies. But other possibilities involving a few radical steps towards the empowerment of local communities might well be explored.

Local communities, as represented by their local authorities, could possibly be allowed to pursue a policy different to that of the government on every single issue; they may even be granted the right to secede and form an independent state, if that is what they want. In the hands of populists, such a right can, of course, prove fatal for both the people concerned and democracy itself. In theory it may even lead to the emergence of new States such as the Islamic Republic of Bradford. But this might well be a risk worth taking, for involvement is meaningful only in undistorted communication with others in a responsive, influenceable and self-regulated society, in the web of life rather than in the web of impersonal bureaucracies. This can only be possible in a small-sized entity.

Facilitating participation in planning and decision-making by the largest possible numbers involves the radical restructuring of institutions to be preceded by the firm rejection of centralisation and the cult of power. In its pursuit, parliamentary democracy cannot be abandoned; public services cannot be allowed to fall apart; and economic considerations cannot be set aside. The 'moneyless, stateless and marketless economy', which Takis Fotopoulos, the Greek political theorist, advocated in his *Towards an Inclusive Democracy*, is far beyond the reach of our culture. Within it, and, indeed, very close to its realisation, is, instead, the cashless world. Politics on a human scale means that the political system needs to be radically transformed with the most powerful groups accepting genuine self-imposed limits so as to allow the less powerful ones to breathe. The task is not technological, as some argue pointing to the Internet, but political. The Internet, though helpful, can decentralise and democratise the world no more than the steam engine did.

Transformation means, for example, that the number of MPs, all non-paid, may increase to a few thousand if all members of the local councils also become members of Parliament. Smaller bodies can scrutinise legislation, but the opinion of an enlarged Parliament would have to be obligatorily taken in all major decisions such as prime minister Blair's decision to join the US war on Iraq. Just in the way British prime minister Gordon Brown established a 'Business Council for Britain' to advise government on all policies affecting business, citizens councils, 'juries' or NGOs can play a consulting role in each government department. They can nominate the peers for the second chamber, if there is to be a second chamber, and also work together with royal commissions to investigate the working of the public and the corporate sector. Pension funds and other shareholders may exert decisively their authority on corporative policy matters, and the Trade Unions, which have for some time now been the hostages of history, may redefine their role, not only as the defenders of workers' rights against corporations and private equity funds, but also as Justice's stewards, defenders of the rights of the weak, guardians of an ethical society. Citizens further can initiate legislation by collecting signatures through the Internet enough to force a referendum.

If the spirit of democracy is the spirit of humanity's best side, democracy needs to challenge Reason as understood by the forces of modernism, and shift the emphasis from profits and wealth to social solidarity. It needs further to question the transformation of the citizen into a member of the market society and of the state into the accomplice of multinationals, and to reject the law of the jungle which underpins the strategic policy concepts of the free market and its politicians. Adherence to human values means acknowledgment of the whole and the rights of all its parts, Justice, on which society's morality needs to rest, balance, proportion and symmetry in life, the appreciation of beauty in all its forms and commitment to the truth even if the latter still looks like a bedraggled victim of a street crime. Freedom demands what Andreas Kalvos, the Greek poet, suggested in one of his immortal lines, *areté kai tólmhi* – virtue and guts.

The current perception of democracy as a neutral force, i.e. a set of procedures and rules, the systematic order which alienates and spreads discord, is the repulsive image of a world jelled together by money, Georg Simmel's 'great leveller' which dissolves bonds based on blood, kinship, solidarity or loyalty. Turned into rules of conduct, it denies its own nature – hospitals in the UK PLC could then be expected to treat only the most profitable diseases. But democracy is not a set of rules. It is, instead, a living organism drawing strength from the daily collective determination of meanings and values in tune with the land's cultural and historical traditions which permeate our living reality and, as it is, in tune also with the new realities of the heterogeneous social order. As such, it respects, or it should, what is not 'us'. It is bound, or it should be, by the links of solidarity which, starting at family level, provide the pattern for the solidarity of the whole society. But it also fights for its truth, it struggles, if I can use Hegelian language, to come into its truth. Democracy, in this sense, is never final. As a living value system, it keeps adjusting to meet the expectations of each new generation.

Readjustments within the institutions are always possible, and relatively easy. But shifting the political emphasis from the individual to the community, re-engaging the citizens in the city's business, and going for a major renewal and revitalization of public life, which many, 'far from the land Greece, beyond the Western stars', as Euripides would say, have campaigned for, is not. The empowerment of local communities by strategies of support, including revenue-sharing and technical assistance, and for the creative use of the structures of civil society has failed to materialise because the task required a major social movement which refused to be born. Despite its appalling consequences, the mercenary pursuit of self-interest in a life cut off from the social, political, economic, or moral order remains as vibrant as the rush hour traffic.

To function the way the Greek polis did, a community needs a common vision of the common good that springs from shared nationality, language, identity, culture, history, religion or a way of life. Only then we will have what Emile Durkheim called 'collective effervescence' – 'the ritually induced passsion or ecstasy that cements social bonds'. But none of these are obtainable in modern cities, where people, having been born on this side of the street, do not know what is on the other. A city like London is no longer 'us', but 'us' and 'them', 'them' being all the different ethnic, religious, racial or cultural groups unified only by the forces of the market. Citizens will identify with the state, Charles Taylor said, but only if there is a 'common form of life' whose preservation matters to them for its own sake and not because of its instrumental use. A citizen can and will be generous if a tsunami hits the coastal cities of Indonesia, but he or she will not easily accept sacrifices, if he needs to make sacrifices, for the benefit of an amorphous, nondescript world.

This is, incidentally, the contradiction in which liberal democracies find themselves, for as long as they place the emphasis on individual rights they dismiss by definition any shared conception of the good. In addition, the idea of community, manipulated historically by totalitarian regimes and vehemently opposed by postmodern individualism, is considered by many as a step in the wrong direction. As professor Will Kymlicka said, in our postmodernist world the politics of difference demands differentiated citizenship which requires recognition of the customs, laws and habits of ethnic, religious and cultural minorities, in other words, the recognition of special rights and claims. But others are sharply opposed to such an approach. Civil society is not by definition the 'seedbed of civic virtue', families are often 'a school in despotism', churches practise manipulation, and ethnic groups may well lack the necessary loyalty to the state and/or be organised in internally illiberal ways. Islamist groups committed to terrorism in the same Western cities where they were born have only strengthened the resolve of many to prevent the disintegration of their community.

John Rawls and Dworkin had tried earlier to solve the problem by suggesting that, whatever their conceptions of the good, the citizens will accept the concept of Justice, i.e., living in an ethical community. But again the difficulty here is that 'Justice' is subject to various interpretations from which escaping is often as easy as escaping one's own gender, and fairness is not as a rule extended to those beyond the borders of any particular interpretation. But, on the other hand, Justice, as a concept, offers the only basis on which modern ethics and contemporary morality can be founded.

The problem is, of course, whose values European democracy is expected to express, those in the European and secular tradition or those of its new and amorphous multiethnic, multireligious and multicultural world. Pluralism, and faith schools which segregate the community and sow alienation, supported for good reason by elements of the Western world's ethnic and religious minorities, protects these minorities' right to be. And democracy as a set of rules, albeit soulless, has no problem with it provided that the minorities accept the mainstream's rules and pay their rent to capitalism.

The right to be different is of fundamental importance in a democratic multicultural society worthy of its name. But its recognition has a price tag attached to it. It can eventually force a country to accept a minority's old-fashioned cultural conservatism which has been decisively rejected by the West, things like religious fundamentalism, marginalisation of women, hostility to homosexuality or unfree education. It can also have a major impact on its political stability, its culture and core values, its social cohesion, even its psyche. But, as Pausanias says in Plato's *Symposium*, social disintegration is not undesirable in tyrannical states because the interests of their rulers require subjects poor in spirit, without strong bonds of friendship or society among them, which love, above all other motives, is likely to inspire. This does not seem applicable to our liberal society but, as Kondylis held, the liberal society on whose behalf the anti-communist crusade was conducted is no longer. Bourgeois modernity has been replaced by a mass democratic postmodernity, i.e. a postliberal society whose dissimilarity from the bourgeois age is greater than the difference between Europe before the French revolution and the Europe of the late nineteenth century. To claim that mass democracy is anything but the fictional continuity with the liberal past is, he said, an ideological misrepresentation.

Author Michael Ignatieff insisted, however, that protection of minority cultures is precisely what distinguishes liberal 'civic nations' from illiberal 'ethnic nations' whose goal is the reproduction of a particular ethnoculture.

The multiculturalist thesis never appealed to me. In the first place, being a Greek national living in the UK, I did not feel I had a right to demand. I was, and I still am, a guest, who, in return for the hospitality I am being offered, has to respect the existing social norms. The bottom line is that I have not been forced by the British to settle in the UK. I settled in London on my own free will, and Britain, therefore, owes me nothing.

Of course, being a white European, I am not in the same situation ethnic minorities are. Although I have occasionally been offered 'sympathy' for being a foreigner, I have never experienced any discrimination against me which, perhaps, makes all the difference. But even so, I could not see why people who choose to come and live in the UK should refuse to integrate into its common societal culture, endorse the basic corpus of shared values and be loyal to the country which gave them a home. Nor could I see why the majority should forego its own identity, accept illiberal minority practices, and live with all the consequences of subcultures, including political alienation, criminality and religious fundamentalism. But, of course, this kind of thinking may well be judged in the context of the prejudices under which my white, European and bourgeois background has damned me to labour. Should that be the case, I am still, however, happy to let its tune dance on my midnight floor.

Otherness is not colourless as the wind and odourless as thoughts. It does not inhabit the land beyond our understandings of good or bad, right or wrong, beautiful or ugly, and it does not, like money, abolish the difference between truth and falsity. Respect for the values of the Other, particularly when Otherness turns into an occupation, demands, therefore, as much as anything else their critical assessment. The battle of ideas has not reached the end of time. Democracy is not emancipated from every value. It is not a system with water in its veins, a supermarket providing good service at affordable prices or a bureaucracy guaranteeing law and order. A nation that asks nothing of its government but the maintenance of law and order, de Tocqueville said at a time similar to our own, is already a slave at heart.

Accepting, respecting, or treasuring otherness is surely vital if we are not to carry on oppressing those who are different from us. After all, one cannot dismiss a fig tree because it does not bear cherries. But the Other, as author Salman Rushdie wrote when talking about the world of Islam, must 'take on board the secularist-humanist principle on which the modern is based'. Without it, 'freedom will remain a distant dream'. Honouring otherness is a manifestation of a wider commitment to humanism, justice and freedom on which respect for otherness rests. There can be no acceptance of otherness if that otherness negates this wider commitment. Equally true, there can be no credible commitment to these principles if their pursuit serves the US-led globalisation and the liberal imperialism's wars.

No Otherness is, in this sense, immune to critical evaluation as long as we are prepared to leave our proud prejudices and all meaner things 'to low ambition and the pride of kings', and make the highest meanings of the world part of the self as much as the highest self a part of the world. The highest in us, Aristotle said, even if it is small in bulk, is still the authoritative part of the self for its power and preciousness far excels the rest.

This 'highest in us', higher than time and as universal as the crying of newborn babies, is, however, better known for the power of its fragility.

9. An Ethical Holism

Preoccupied with security against threats generated by the system itself, and alienated from the whole, whether the whole is the natural world, the inhabitants of this planet, our immediate environment or parts of our own self, we watch, powerless, over the destruction of every image of the whole. The only thing that matters is 'us' as opposed to 'them', whether this 'us' is humans versus the non-human world, economic growth versus nature, the First World versus the Third, modernity versus tradition, the individual versus society, the mind versus the body. This 'us', into which we are hooked twenty-four hours a day, seven days a week, can, indeed, be anything: the cool, white, middle class Britain, the male, heterosexual, Manchester United society, or, to use James Joyce's rather unkind description of the 'brutish' British Empire, a compendium of 'beer, beef, business, bibles, bulldogs, battleships, buggery and bishops'. Whatever, it is always the 'me, me, me' versus the entire world.

Unsinkable as the Titanic and defined in relation to 'them' or 'it', this 'me' delineates everything which involves interaction with our world. It determines our perceptions of reality, the interpretation of our interests, notions of expediency, understandings of necessity, beliefs in ideas and evaluations of beauty though the latter is only taught in history classes as nothing is any longer intrinsically valued. It also defines our relation with the parts of ourselves from which we have disidentified, the aspects of ourselves we no longer recognise as 'us'. Rather than a network of human relationships in which individuals find everything in and through each other, life has subjectively and objectively been transformed into relations, often made and spent like fortunes overnight, between entities with no intrinsic value or connections. How to identify aliens seems under the circumstances no longer to be a problem. We only need to take a look at the person who comes to meet us in the mirror.

The void in the eyes of modernism had become the critical focus of the socialist humanists – Ernst Bloch, Herbert Marcuse, Henri Lefebvre, Murray Bookchin, Costas Axelos, E.P. Thompson, Raymond Williams, Pierre Bourdieu, Jürgen Habermas, Cornelius Castoriades and many others. Focusing on the early writings of Marx and also those of Georg Lukács, Karl Korsch and Antonio Gramsci, they were able to look east of joy and west of pain, and, thus, reopen the old Greek concerns regarding the essence of being human. So did the Austrian psychiatrist Wilhelm Reich, who asked for the abolition of the Judaeo-Christian moral economy, crooked as a dog's leg, in favour of sexual freedom as the necessary condition for all emancipation.

By doing so, they all challenged capitalism on account of its dehumanising practices, the alienation of the human being from his entire world through a process of quantification and abstractification that has transcended the economic sphere and spread to life itself. It was this wing of Marxism that moved towards the ultimate frontiers of *aletheia*, the truth which the Greeks had sought in a self undivided from itself and its world. Defining in this respect was *History and Class Consciousness*, the work of Georg Lukács which was published in Vienna in 1923 to be denounced by the Soviet hierarchy as deviationist and then repudiated by Lukács himself in 1930 for its 'subjectivism' and its 'messianic Utopianism'. Translated into French in 1960 and, thus, crossing the bridge of silence, this book was subsequently heralded by what was called Western Marxism as the touchstone of Marxist humanism – Marx's early writings had not appeared in print as yet.

Just like the early Marx, Lukács shifted the focus of Marxism to the 'dialectical relation between the subject and the object'. Capitalism's 'mechanised rationalisation' of the economy and the conquest of nature, he held, ended in man's alienation from his world. Calculation embraced all aspects of life, and life was reified – reification is the process by which man's own activity controls him by virtue of an autonomy alien to him. Lukács called for an end to the private ownership of the means of production as the only way to end human alienation and the 'reified structure of existence'. The goal, as for the young, the 'Greek' Marx, was the realisation of man's 'authentic humanity' and the development of his 'total personality', the attainment of *areté*. Lucien Goldmann, a pupil of Lukács, articulated the concept further and also linked it to Jean Piaget's developmental psychology. A new Marxism as a 'practical philosophy of freedom' had emerged.

Marx's 'total man', Maximilien Rubel, a social theorist, held, landmarked the emerging new Marxist ethic the focus of which was to end alienation and appropriate man's 'universal being'. The concept of 'total man', the whole man, Henri Lefebvre, the French sociologist, said, refuted all partial views of man such as the Christian man or the economic man.

The man's wholeness, which rests on balance, proportion and symmetry, is the individual's *areté* requiring the exploration of all human potentials and the all-sided development of the human being – mind, body and spirit – in harmony with nature and the community. Being the individual's march to perfection, human rather than economic growth, as taught by Socrates who learned how to play the lyre in his old age, is also the road to personal happiness, the individual's *eudaemonia* which money can never buy. In an imperfect world, happiness can, however, be rather elusive. In downbeat mood, the chorus in Sophocles King Œdipus, thus, wonders whether there is 'the man whose happiness is something more than an illusion'.

Further revising Marxist orthodoxy, Lefebvre considered that economic alienation did not linearly determine alienation in other structures of life since they were all reciprocally interrelated. At the heart of all alienation, whether economic, social or ideological, Costas Axelos, a Greek independent thinker also held, is the alienation of the human being. Orthodox Marxism had sidelined the humans. Western Marxism brought them back into focus.

Incidentally, Axelos noted that Marx had neither specified the origins of alienation, which for Axelos himself are to be traced back to the time when man interposed a tool between himself and the bosom of Mother Nature; nor had he described a past, non-alienated social structure. The omission led rather discomfitingly to the conclusion that man has never been a self-determined agent, in which case alienation is permanent, a part of the human condition. As problematic was Marx's inference that all alienations would permanently end with the triumph of communism, which is just another version of 'the end of history' thesis. The visionary strain in

Marx, Axelos said, could only be understood as 'Jewish prophetism', a prolongation of Western metaphysics, for history will not have the 'happy end' which Marx predicted.

Axelos' chilling vision of the future was continuing alienation originating from the gigantic development of technology from which, ironically, Marx himself expected the salvation. Rather than liberate man and create the fully integrated and all-round individual, Axelos held, soulless technology will create only a sterile, bland, technical wasteland. If history comprises the unravelling of human potential, the growing technopower of humankind makes the actualisation of these nasty potentials even more horrible. Along similar lines, another Greek philosopher, Panajotis Kondylis, saw in Marx's normative-eschatological unification of world history the intensification of the war against social cohesion.

Existentialism's inward looking had, in the meantime, been moderated by Jean-Paul Sartre and Maurice Merleau-Ponty who tried to bridge the gap between existentialism and Marxism by politicising the personal and personalising the political. The American offshoot of this new movement was Humanistic Psychology, psychology's 'Third Force' after psychoanalysis and behaviourism, pioneered by Abraham Maslow, Erich Fromm and Carl Rogers. The angst of an individual 'swallowed up in the infinite ocean of being', his alienation, was again the key word; so was the call for the individual's self-actualisation as perceived by the Greeks. The movement remained, however, rather marginal and ineffective: helping the individual to rediscover himself in, and readjust to society may be useful but not very useful when the values of this society remain unquestioned by the Third Force's practitioners.

Yet 'men', as D.H. Lawrence argued, 'are free when they belong to a living, organic, believing community, active in fulfilling some unfulfilled, perhaps unrealised purpose'. This was for him the path to personal liberation from a system that debases human purpose to 'sheer mechanical materialism' and destroys 'the instinct of community'. Together with an identity, this is also what religion gives to people in a world that has lost all other meaning and connections. The same view was held by Herbert Marcuse, the Frankfurt School theorist, who refused to see personal autonomy in personal terms only; Rudolf Bahro, the German Green philosopher, who looked forward to the reintegration of man into communal life; Murray Bookchin, the leading American social thinker, who insisted that individuality is inseparable from community; or Jürgen Habermas, for whom the common ground is the higher-order subjectless intersubjectivity.

This common ground, Habermas explained in his idiosyncratic language which to illuminate you need a lamp with triple flame, is centred in a civil society, which yields a normative model in which 'the socially integrative force of solidarity ... develops in widely differentiated autonomous public spheres and legally institutionalised procedures of democratic opinion and will-formation so that it can also hold its own against the other two mechanisms of social integration: money and administrative power'.

Historically, the whole has never been dismissed, except that, when acknowledged, it was more often than not blessed with rights exclusively conferred upon 'us' by God, nature, history and various other high sounding nonsensicalities of the blood-and-soil ideology which ostensibly give flesh to the collective will. The evil, the brutal, and oppressive reality this, presumably, exclusive contract between the truth and its violent lovers has produced is only too well documented by the centuries' extremism whose account, so embarrassing that we would rather not know, tends sometimes to sound like the confessions of an amnesiac. This 'whole', to which postmodernism rightly objects, is a violation of the right of everything to be free within the context of the whole, respected by, and respectful of, it; a tyranny which has led to the destruction of the whole in its very name. Perceived in mythical, racial or nationalistic terms, it is only the totalitarians' spiritual supplement taken in doses proportional to their savagery.

Liberation from oppression does not require, however, the

fragmentation of the whole, with each group, like each individual, pursuing its own interests regardless of what happens to the others and the rest of the world. The One may have its internal oppositions but this does not mean it is not in harmony with itself just, Heraclitus said, as the lyre is when its pulsating chords move in opposing directions in a synthetic rather than a dialytic manner. The whole, as encapsulated by Logos, the voice of all its parts and their connections, interdependencies and oppositions, is not committed to domination, but, just like the spring, to the right of everything to be. Diversity in unity is its very essence.

Relations between its many elements are as important as the elements themselves whose needs are balanced against those of the other in a spirit of compromise dictated by the acceptance of self-imposed limits. On this depends the integrity of the elements themselves and also the functionality of the whole and the strength of the chain which cannot be broken without courting disaster. This is obvious in the case of abuses – abuses such as of rights, alcohol or sleeplessness – which disturb the whole, which, unwilling to tolerate iniquities to its constituent parts, reacts violently to reassert itself.

'Us' and 'them', distinct from each other are not expected to live lovingly with each other. Cooperation is in nature, but so is competition, which, as Freud said, will continue even if all social and economic reasons for it disappear. It can continue even after life as shown by Mopsus and Amphilochus, who, rather than accept that, being dead, they had become inoperative, set up a new oracle business in direct competition to Delphi. The responses, incidentally, were given in dreams at the remarkably low price of two coppers apiece.

Strife within the whole will, indeed, never end as no party to it either can, or should be able to, win, control and dominate, elbow out of existence or eliminate its opposition. To do so would disturb the delicate balance of the whole and offend some sort of eternal order which has given everything its place. Exception to this rule, Hesiod tells us, was made only once, when Zeus, impersonating

Amphitryon, lay with his wife Alcmene one ambrosial night to which he gave the length of three. Helios, the Sun, although grumbling about the good old times when day was day and night was night, had agreed to oblige.

Going back to the initial assumptions, the premise of Logos, is to remind ourselves of the connection of everything that is, mind and feelings, body and soul, the mundane and the sacred, the individual and the community. It is what bridges all dualities, the personal and the political, culture and nature, appearance and reality, contingent and universal, town and country, thought and labour, man and woman, reality and dream, rights and responsibilities. We do not just laugh, we also cry, though still only privately as capitalism has not as yet created places for mass weeping.

10. Some 'Normal' Assumptions

Being a part of our world rather than its visitor implies that nature is our homeland rather than enemy territory and as such it has to be respected, the world's limited resources are there for the benefit of all rather than the richest 2 per cent of the world which owns more than 50 per cent of global assets, and the community is the extended family rather than the terminator of our individuality. In the same way, the emotional, sensual and spiritual parts of ourselves complement rather than antagonise our mind; science and technology serve the whole rather than their paymasters; education, in a world in which we know less every day, trains people as good human beings and citizens rather than functionaries with brains clogged with useless data.

The concept, which wears its years with distinction, rules out excesses by definition, particularly excesses in pleasure, which

Aristotle thought are licentious, and a culpable thing. Excess is, of course, easily recognised in the case of alcoholism, ludicrous diets, drug dependencies, abuse of rights in certain situations, or suppression of the will of the whole, particularly if effected by the force of arms. But it is also inherent in religious fundamentalism, Islamist or otherwise, which by calling for a return to the second age of the West, the religious, is determined to deny humankind the pleasures of life, even life itself.

Nevertheless, definite assumptions as to what is 'normal', on the strength of which we determine what is 'excess', cannot easily be made. Normality does not seem to come naturally to our world. Indeed, a commonly accepted criterion of normality is lacking in most cases. We know for example, for certain that fever is an indication of ill-health or that smoking kills. But we do not know in the same way that roads built only for cars are an indication of defective thinking, or that loneliness, the condition in which, as Byron would say, none is left to please because none is left to love, has the same effects as smoking. My argument that the current crisis is primarily a cultural and spiritual one has nothing of the force inherent in almost any medical diagnosis.

I would, of course, be on much safer ground if I were to argue that we are not doing so well because the country's exports are not doing so well. But then, as historian and social critic R. H. Tawney would have rightly said, I would have confused one minor department of life with the whole.

Just like truth and falsity, normality and deviation from it, often socially construed, are concepts impossible to determine objectively. The night used to be the time people rested in order to cope with the demands of life in the day, but this is no longer the case. Divorce or homosexuality used, likewise, to be seen as deviations from what was believed to be a normal life, but this too obtains no longer. Even confirming objectively that we age is not possible in the age of Viagra and Protect & Perfect Beauty Serum. Rather than fixed and immutable, normality, representing the totality of historically determined relations whose content and logical formulation must be seen, as Gramsci argued in *The Modern Prince*, as a developing organism, keeps evolving. Yet, despite all uncertainties, or uncertain certainties, the multi-interpretability of all scenarios, we all know that anything that harms us, physically, mentally or emotionally, cannot be normal, in which case we all look forward to a return to normality. The latter does, therefore, exist in some form or substance.

It requires both stability and change, time spent in social interaction, but also time for ourselves, good decisions, but also proper consultation with all people who are to be affected by those decisions. It rests on attention to both the visible and the invisible parts of our existence as well as the measurable and the non-measurable ones; and it sets limits, those which define the concept of the right and the good. In its Greek sense, it is love for beauty which rules out excess, from diet and work to town planning and foreign policy. What the whole cannot accept is fragmentation leading to exclusion. This ethicality, brought into the human realm, gave birth to natural rights, the rights of man, and ensured among other things that democracy is the political system blessed by nature.

The holistic views are, nevertheless, dismissed by rigid orthodoxies, ludicrous specialisations, and collective obsessions, whose artless countenance and mutual incompatibility, Arthur Koestler said, is reflected in a 'controlled schizophrenia'. The whole, though it has shaped our perceptions, is no longer graspable. It does not even exist – presumably it died without even knowing it and was absent from its own funeral which never took place.

The system is not interested in the happiness of the individual but only in his efficiency as a worker. It is not concerned about the environment but only about economic growth; and it does not care about the wellbeing of the community but only about its spending power. The free marketeers, valuing individual choice to which all other goods are subordinated, are only too happy to let the market take care of our needs as speedily as possible. The liberals, who claim that a substantive and unifying vision of the common good is incompatible with pluralism, give this understanding the intellectual respectability it requires; and the postmodernists refuse to accept the existence of the 'totalising', even 'terrorist', as former champion of the Trotskyist *Socialisme ou Barbarie* Jean-François Lyotard said, philosophy of holism and its ideal of consensus. The whole is no longer. 'Segius said the skies are empty and the gods are dead', Martial, the Latin epigrammatist, had succinctly said nearly twenty centuries ago; 'proof of it is that he sees himself made rich'. The future, designed by the current individualistic common sense, is obviously more powerful than love.

Here I can, however, hear Raymond Tallis, the neurologist, reproaching me, as he reproached so many other 'hysterical humanists', with the precise words 'there you go again, summarising India'. His book, subtitled *A Critique of Contemporary Pessimism*, was very popular as a doorstop.

Faced with a disintegrating world, attempts to bring back holism, the oneness of it all, as the guiding principle of action are anything but lacking. But the attempts, missing their target, leave behind only the odour of their failure. The New Age, like the Gnostics in earlier times, sees the whole in quasi-religious terms – oneness as union with some sort of a higher consciousness. The task, metaphysical, is, therefore, to get in touch, and identify, with it in splendid isolation from what most people, those who still perspire, would call reality. In the very name of holism, New Age holism ends up as monism inhabiting a private vacuum, sighing in tune with some sort of cosmic energy and possessing an eerie quality almost suggestive of a seance.

The free market economy, which, like Jane Austen's Mrs Bennet, 'a woman of mean understanding, little information, and uncertain temper', is, likewise, inclinable with a rather hurried earnestness towards the holistic concept, the latest in thinking. But what appeals to it is its rationalism only – not the morality and the ethos it embodies. Rationalistic holism, accepting the bleedingly obvious, i.e. the simple fact that nothing exists in isolation, recognises the importance of the whole environment in which business activities grow. 'Economic life', Francis Fukuyama argued in his *Trust*, 'is deeply embedded in social life, and cannot be understood apart from the customs, morals and habits of the society in which it occurs. In short, it cannot be divorced from culture'.

The whole, James Wolfensohn, former president of the World Bank, acknowledged for his part, is the financial, institutional and social together. The 'holistic' approach to promoting development, he told his staff, has to reflect an analytical framework which grants other aspects, structural, social and human, equal status to the macroeconomic. The Other aspects include good government, vigorous anti-corruption policies, a social safety net, education, health, access to energy, communications, protection of the environment and preservation of cultural heritage. Others stressed, likewise, that nations are not merely economic units but also societies tied together by social compacts explicit in laws and implicit in behaviour considered morally acceptable.

In this spirit, the United Nations has endorsed a holistic birth control plan, town planners talk about the need for holistic urban development or the EU promotes a holistic approach to integrated coastal zone management. Even Scotland Yard, as its spokesman said once on television, looks forward to a holistic approach to crime – David Blunkett, at the time the UK's Home Secretary, asserted, too, that his nationality, migration, and asylum policy was to be 'holistic', presumably with a hole in it, a *Daily Telegraph* columnist explained rather acidly.

Yet holism remains an undigested theory, a shadow detached from its body. Industry needs to be 'holistic', the Cambridge Technology Centre pronounced, except that, as it explained, holism means 'developing or redesigning factories for total productivity (i.e. lowest cost of total employees)'. Likewise, as toiletries and fragrances for babies have turned into a big business, mothers are now invited to address the wellbeing and skincare problems of the 'whole' baby

– perhaps, *Petit Guerlain Eau de Senteur* for £30 or *Bulgari pour Petit et Maman* for £40 will do; other 'life-enhancing' lotions are also available. Life is important only in terms of what sells.

The only area in which holism has really gained a measure of acceptance is medicine. Complementary therapies have successfully questioned the fundamentally reductionist medical practice which breaks the body into organs and parts. Their model is, instead, the Hippocratic one which treats the body as a whole and as a part of its physical and social environment. This is a model which even orthodox medicine is currently being forced to accept when, in order to understand and cure the organ, it builds bridges between molecules and systems, genetic features, lifestyles, social and environmental factors, even whole ecosystems. But overall, holism, the alternative to the capitalist material monoculture, hijacked, distorted and demasculinised, has turned into a gala performance for the benefit of all those who insure their taste against misappropriation and, in John Lennon's immortal words, 'rattle (their) jewellery' in approval.

The 'holistic' approach to development reflects the whole as much as water reflects images, i.e. without absorbing them. It contains nothing but itself.

11. Perfect in its Vagueness

Morality for the Greeks meant Justice. The latter, which should be at the heart of every beginning, requires the recognition of everyone's right to live in peace, free from fear, domination, manipulation, abasement and exploitation. Justice, Jürgen Habermas said, demands the greatest possible equality of subjective freedoms, membership in a free association of citizens, actionable rights and individual legal protection, equal rights to processes of opinion and will-formation, and rights to a life socially, technically and ecologically secure. This is our right to security of existence in life's wintry streets, protected against avoidable risks, able to develop to the best of our abilities and pursue our own goals, and free to enjoy, as much as rain falling in dry wine, all the simple pleasures of life.

Even if, to quote Italian filmmaker Pier Paolo Pasolini, as poor as a cat in the Colosseum, we all have a right to clean air and water, respect for who and what we are, active membership in the human club, a voice in the way our common affairs are run, and a friendly smile. We all also have the right to be kissed tenderly at night or to make enough mistakes to enjoy life to the full.

Yet man cannot be full of self-importance. 'I come from the countryside', Lorca said, 'and I do not believe that man is the most important thing in the world'. This requires respect by all, including those who have visited only the countryside's website instead of the countryside itself, for all living things on earth, the Greeks' 'Mother of all life'. It calls for appreciation of everything that is on the planet – its seas, mountains, valleys, rivers and all creatures great and small. It also demands care so that the world is a good place for both 'us' and 'them' and safe enough for both the present and future generations. When this uninjured awareness comes into consciousness, nothing needs to prove its importance. Everything has a purpose determined by its very existence rather than those 'whose hearts are dry as summer dust', as William Wordsworth put it only to hear his words' echo in a vacuum because either the audience was not there or it did not play its part.

The recognition that everything, human and non-human, has its rightful place in the world which needs to be gracefully acknowledged, respected and protected may well be out of tune with our time – and not only our time. When postmodernism was introduced in Greece at the end of the great era, Thrasymachus, the Sophist, argued brutally that people consider it is right or noble to respect other people's interests only because someone else has greater power over them. Yet, respect for what is not 'us' is the supreme moral law, the essence of Justice, which, going beyond the needs of humans within their socioeconomic context only, and, of course, beyond the awry Christian morality, ensures that the sun shines for all without discrimination. Whatever is not 'us' is not a means to increase 'our' wealth and power, but something with intrinsic value worthy of our protection. I like to think of it as if it had a soul, as if 'God' was in it.

Morality has nothing to do with a person's sexuality, which, as the power that can cross all boundaries, has been at the very heart of the division between a secular humanistic culture and its theocratic, heteronomous, and by definition, anti-humanist equivalent embedded in the historical split between Athens and Jerusalem. It relates only to fairness, and fairness demands that we deal fairly with everyone and everything: the members of our family and our friends, our employers or employees, suppliers and customers, leaders and supporters, our community. But it also means dealing fairly with the rivers and the seas, the forests and the animals, the world, future generations, and, finally, our own selves; also with me when reading this book, for, I hope, you will not focus only on my mistakes! Everything that is not 'us', if 'us' is humans, males, Europeans, the young, or the able-bodied is still part of 'us', even when it does not have a voice to express its anguish, and even when we, blindly, at home with our misery, fail to see it and identify with it. For inside 'their' distress lies a portion of our own.

Poet Odysseus Elytis' fear that he 'might break a flower, or hurt a bird and so put God in a difficult position', makes the case beautifully for man's total responsibility. But it also makes the case for the universality of Justice, if Justice means care for everybody and everything, protection of their right to exist free of fear, the fear that threatens one's very existence. This, which cannot be legislated, demands personal attributes – fair-mindedness, honesty and courage, in rather short supply in our time – and now and then a glass of wisdom.

One does, of course, have to make allowances for the 'context' and the inclemencies of history, but, on the other hand, whatever the context, if asked, seagulls will never agree to die on oil-polluted beaches, monkeys will never acquiesce to ending their lives painfully in laboratories, forests will never permit their destruction by man. No person loves living in fear, no hungry, homeless, destitute people will ever concur with their condition, no repressed individuals, minorities or nations will salute their repression. Likewise, no homosexual man or woman will accept his or her being bullied, no one will endorse his or her being racially discriminated against, no person will ever forego his or her right to be, and no culture or language will ever commit suicide. Nonetheless, people and situations are forced to submit to a power which places no limits on itself, coerced to accept what they do not want to accept and consent to their exploitation, repression or destruction.

To me, this defines the universality of injustice, recognised, as Aristotle said, like the unsound condition of the body, the injury inflicted on its parts. As such, it sets the parameters within which universal Justice can be explored, and humanism as the 'actual appropriation of the human essence' according to Marx or the 'endeavour to render man free for – and to find dignity in – his humanity' according to Heidegger can be given flesh.

Trying to embody the hopes and aspirations of the whole of humanity rather than those reflecting class, gender, race or other interests, morality as a universal concept needs no other justification than ourselves as long as we are willing to access our rational mind and intuitive sense and as long as society both encourages and educates us to live in harmony with our higher aspirations. The principles of Justice, John Rawls said, are not something which we 'discover' or of which we 'become aware', but something which we cannot but postulate when we intuitively try to work out what is right and wrong. Though imperfect in its vagueness, this may not provide universally shared values to which the citizens of the world will be invited to subscribe. If nothing else, conflicting interests will never allow it. Judiciously virile, it gives, however, protection to concerns currently unprotected, and de-legitimises the postmodernist approach according to which judgment, like art, obeys no law other than its own. High-mindedness seems, however, to be the prerogative of the rich as the poor cannot afford it.

Nevertheless, the issue is not as complicated as subject-centered philosophy would have us believe, for, after all, whether good or bad, the rain is still wet. It is not technical, either, the province of experts, all those who, fighting the modern threats which often they themselves have created, seem determined to deprive us of our democratic freedoms. Indeed, we do not need an expert with a professorial face to tell us that freedom and security of existence are what a civilised society is expected to provide to its members just as we do not need an expert to tell us that the medical profession's job is to cure a medical condition. In any given society, and although our consciousness interprets the given world as much as it reflects it, the ends, though always transmutable, are, somehow, determined. This means that as much as we are all entitled to enjoy in idle innocence the honey-gold serenity of a mid-summer afternoon, we all deserve, likewise, to be able to enjoy at least the minimum of what is socially validated as good.

Understood this way, morality provides, of course, an answer which is no better than the irritating advice given by the pythoness to Podaleirius to look for safety wherever he would suffer no harm even if the skies were to fall. It does not inform us what the nature of womanhood is, and it does not give an authoritative answer to questions about euthanasia, abortion, the cloning of human embryos for research purposes, or the death penalty. Likewise, it fails to guide us as to the desirable level of taxation, it tells us nothing about single parenthood, and it does not speak with one voice when it comes to issues such as genetically modified crops, the single currency or nuclear power, 'the clean and safe answer to the US energy crisis' according to US president George W. Bush. The same moral law can itself be legitimately questioned, too, for the protection of the right of everyone and everything to be cannot, presumably, be extended to cover what is harmful to the 'whole'.

'Rats and mice, flies and frogs and bugs and lice' have been given a place in this world, and, though encumbered with physical disadvantages vis-à-vis the humans, defend their existence as vigorously as humans do their own. Still humans, unimpressed, looking after their own interests, do their best to eradicate. But, perhaps, in this case, as Aristotle said, a thing whose presence or absence makes no visible difference is not an organic part of the whole. As questionable is the meaning of the word 'harmful' or the legitimacy of action against the enemies of the 'whole', if the 'whole' is defined by the cathedrals of power which exclude all those who do not share 'our' values.

Full and equal distribution of everything, wealth, honours, dignity, in the name of social justice has, of course, as much of a chance of making it as a snowball in the seventh circle of hell. Fundamentally, the concept has its own internal limitations, for nature, refusing to progress or regress like her subjects, cannot, or is unwilling to, distribute her favours equally to everybody; and merit, as Aristotle said, has to be rewarded. Still, the mark of a moral, civilised society is the care it takes of everybody, and this is the premise on which John Rawls' liberal thesis on Justice, most influential until the Reagan–Thatcher era, rests. His Aristotelian 'justice as fairness' approach acknowledges the principle of equal rights, liberties and also duties. 'Each person', he said, 'is to have an equal right to the most extensive total system of equal basic liberties compatible with a similar system of liberty for all'. His system makes room for inequalities if they help the least advantaged, or, according to the British Labour Party social thinker Anthony Crosland, if they advance the interests of the community.

Raymond Williams, following to some extent in the steps of Coleridge and Ruskin, changed the emphasis in the argument. Endorsing an understanding of equality in a humanistic context, he argued that the only essential, or indeed conceivable, equality is equality of being. Inequality of being rejects, degrades, depersonalises the human being, cripples human energy, harbours domination, cruelty and exploitation, and extinguishes moral instinct. R.H. Tawney, the British socialist theorist, had already elegantly argued that a society is civilised only insofar as it uses its material resources to promote 'the dignity and refinement of the individual human beings who compose it'.

This aspiration goes, however, beyond what Ronald Dworkin, the 'Third Way' philosophical guru, can entertain. For him all a society needs to show is equal concern for its citizens. 'Equal concern', he said, 'is the sovereign virtue of political community', involving, however, action to minimise disparities in wealth or access to resources. Robert Nozick, the Harvard University professor, offered, likewise, another narrow interpretation of Justice in favour of the legitimate ownership of assets. 'The holdings of a person', he said, 'are just if he is entitled to them by the principles of justice in acquisition and transfer'. Inequality here is dressed up in clothes designed to win ethical respectability.

Incidentally, the notion of equality was not so dear to Marx's heart. Hence his ideal, communist, society rested on the principle 'to everyone according to his needs'. The equal distribution of burdens and benefits could not, therefore, meet the individuals' different needs and priorities. As R. H. Tawney pointed out, equality of provision is not identity of provision; equality is achieved only by ensuring that needs are met in different ways, the most appropriate in each case. However, the perennial question of how to satisfy people who want equality but hate being equals to everybody else is still unanswered.

Distributive justice is, however, anathema to those who, like William Dobbin in Thackeray's *Vanity Fair*, are addicted to selfish calculation, the free marketeers. As Friedrich Hayek, the Austrian-born British economist, stated, the principles society should be run on are better left to the market. Social justice, he claimed, is elusive as a concept, and stability and integration of contemporary society tends to rest, not on shared values, but on market mechanisms – for others, it rests on some functional or systemic interdependence. Still, the free market revolution has been able to set the contemporary political agenda. Although the so-called 'Third Way' has not exactly denounced equality as a chimerical concept, it has in effect abandoned it completely; and equality, as a cardinal political virtue, has now the looks of a blasted tree. Rather than Justice, the middle classes' object of desire is, instead, the new Ferrari 360 Modena Spider or the latest Louis Vuitton ostrich skin hold-all handbag.

The contractual theory of Justice, a social-democratic model, was opposed, not only by the free marketeers, but also by those who consider that it advances Kantian, universalistic concepts incongruous to our new, 'decentred' world. Nevertheless, if such a moral law fails to be universally acknowledged as such, and 'the glasses of injustice' continue to be 'foaming', this has much less to do with the presumed decentredness of our world and much more with our own failure to see Justice as a virtue to which we will adhere rather than pay lip service. Corporations, which are trying to project an image of themselves as caring about the social and environmental impact of their business, know very well what an ethical policy involves. Still, they honour it in its betrayal rather than in its observance; and injustice, which, Plato held, 'is always an evil and a dishonour to him who acts unjustly', is done, not out of difficulty to tell what Justice is about, but out of the most radiant indifference to its calls.

The system, Richard Sennett, sociology Professor at New York University said rather charitably in his book *The Corrosion of Character*, 'radiates indifference'. It takes no interest in the fate of the world. As in a Henri Bergson story, in which the visitor did not weep at a sermon when everybody else was shedding tears, he answered when he was asked why he did not: 'I don't belong to the parish'. Corporations, like the visitor, do not seem to belong to the human race.

Hence Heraclitus' understanding of Justice had nothing to do with 'love'. 'Justice', he said, 'is strife', 'war', so that all things come about in accordance 'with what they must be'. Wars and battles may seem terrible, but, as Porphyry, the Neoplatonist philosopher, explaining Heraclitus' views said, 'they all contribute to the harmony of the universe, managing it commodiously'.

Capitalist inequality makes little allowance for liberal or Marxist thinking. Politically, its equality is what Karl Mannheim called 'negative democratisation', occurring when a number of individuals are equally subject to one individual and, thereby, equal among themselves. And socially, equality, offered by the standardised market, is the negative equality which treats humanity like a herd and feeds it cotton balls soaked in grease. Rather than being equal in strength, individuals are equal in their weakness and rather than being equal as distinct individuals, with their own diacritical marks, they are equal in their sameness. Likewise, rather than being equal in joy, they are equal in misery. Agnes, Milan Kundera's character in his novel *Immortality*, covers her ears to protect herself against the noise of pneumatic drills which are pounding the asphalt, and a passer-by gives her an angry glance and taps his forehead – you must be crazy. She had no right to cover her ears. It was not the man but 'equality itself which reprimanded her for refusing to undergo what everyone must undergo'. Zeus himself would have shared the same fate if, as Palladas of Alexandria said, 'he'd been human and poor'.

Wisdom does not reside in other, faraway lands, inaccessible until now. Nor does it demand powers we never had. Not all powers have to be discovered, John Fowles said in his mesmerising *The Magus*; some have to be regained. Nevertheless, searching for the essentials which will enable us to reconnect with the generous, benevolent and noble part of ourselves is bound to look like a journey to the other side of eternity. Yet this is the journey which can break through all barriers of the self and take us back on the road to some sort of original purity.

But, as Zeus decreed some time ago, man must suffer to be wise.

12. The 'Right Thing'

The madness of Reason, as Reason is understood by modernism, overrides institutions and cannot be controlled through changes in the law for which whatever is legal is right, moral and fair. This is the case even if the law is determined to impose several external limitations to reduce the impact of human destructiveness carried out in the name of 'progress', 'growth', 'civilisation', 'democracy' or 'freedom'. Stupidity, ambition, greed or envy, the demands of an Ego, the governing part of our personality, that is unwilling to acknowledge that anything apart from the precious 'me' exists, cannot be controlled by decrees. Unique individuals, undistinguishable from each other, will do anything they can to increase the benefits they are entitled to on account of their 'uniqueness'.

External controls of man's destructiveness are always possible. But nobody but one's own self can force the agent to accept internal checks and balances, act with self-restraint, acknowledge the rights of the 'Other', and put in place a set of useful self-limitations. The issue, though personal, is at the same time political in a broad sense, for our entire culture, founded on the freedoms of the individual as opposed to those of anything or anybody else, does not even understand the needs of the individual it represents. Utilitarianism has turned everything into a means to an end, which is the domination of everything and the accumulation of more wealth, power and influence. The only thing that matters in its realm are results assessed by a calculating machine, known also as the 'mind', honoured to the exclusion of the other constituent parts of the self. Character-building or the quest of the soul for meaning, the emotional truth Faust or Don Giovanni were so desperately looking for, are all dismissed as unimportant.

The external has fully ostracised the internal, and madness, always able to appear with a refreshed smile, continues to reign supreme even in our daily, enervating, mundane routines. But, though damaged, we, somehow, manage to survive it. Human beings, Myrivilis, the Greek novelist, suggested, possess an inexhaustible inner reserve of adaptive capability which rescues them from great misfortunes and especially from madness.

Good can never be good enough if it does not reflect indispensable qualities of the inner self. Inner and outer are not two sovereign republics, sometimes interconnected, but nevertheless always separate from each other. They are, instead, part of the One in constant dialogue with each other, affecting each other even when the dialogue seems to be conducted between the deaf. But inner awakening through self-scanning is not the business of civil society but of specialised agencies such as the Church or psychoanalysis whose founders did, admittedly, try to make a difference.

Awareness, Erich Fromm said, is a condition of winning freedom, the freedom to choose well with reverence for life, the freedom which can be achieved only in unity with people and in rational social action. The latter is necessary as the individual is confronted not by his own uncertainties only, but also by the soul-disfiguring consumerism and the commodification of our existence, the compartmentalisation and sullen loneliness of a hectic life, the alienation from the world, the powerlessnes which has transformed us all into pathetic spectators of life as shown on TV, or the demands of a society dedicated, as T.S. Eliot said, to the pursuit of money and profit. The individual is overpowered, too, as Turkish novelist Orhan Pamuk, the Nobel prize winner charged in Turkey for 'insulting Turkishness', put it, by his inability to make his voice, heavily accented by tiredness, heard, the failure to be understood, the feelings of impotence.

But the radicalism of the 'Third Force', which saw in therapy the means to reconnect the individual with meaning in a social and also political context, just as that of Freud, which confronted the individual with the repressed desires of his or her unconscious, or of Wilhelm Reich and Jacques Lacan which linked, although in very different ways, the personality and its distortions to a repressive social and political or linguistic and cultural order, is often flattened out by its practitioners. Erich Fromm did say so in so many words when he exclaimed tearfully over his Evian that psychology betrays the fundamental lack of human interaction in human relations. Psychological knowledge becomes a substitute for full knowledge in the act of love, instead of being a step towards it. As the word 'psychiatrist' frightens everybody who is not rich, the acknowledgement may well have brought some relief to many.

However, as Aristotle pointed out, a society can only be as good as its members just as a state is as good as its citizens. In his time, each individual had, therefore, to be good, for the polis depended on it. At the same time, the goodness of all was necessary for the goodness of each. Hence individual goodness was not the task of the individual alone. The polis itself, breathing concern about its destiny, had to consider how a man could become and also remain a good man. The Greeks solved the problem by placing the emphasis on *paideia*, the education of the young in the spirit of *areté*, crucial to their elevation and ennoblement. Education of the youngsters was not a profession, but the citizens' moral duty discharged with delight on every single occasion until, of course, the arrival of the sophists who turned education into a well-paid job. The citizens and the polis itself supported the individual in the making of the right choices, and the assumptions made could not be easily challenged. Still the just and honourable life, doing what Plato called 'the right thing', was, ultimately, the choice of the individual.

The 'right thing' was defined by Reason alone. But Reason was Logos: intelligence at one with morality, calculation at one with intuition, and logic at one with human passions. As Democritus said, guarding against injustice is primarily 'the mark of good sense'. 'Nourished and rooted within man', this good sense is the manifestation both of man's good nature and of his understanding of his own interests. Justice is, in this sense, Reason itself, identified with man's intelligent and natural disposition towards an ethical life. Acting against it defeats what matters most to the individual. Doing the 'right thing' expresses, thus, an explicit and articulate grasp of principle, and represents the choice of the rational mind for which good means Reason and Reason means good. Morality, as a concept, cannot, therefore, be exterior to the self, as Christianity pronounced later. It resides in us, and, determined by Logos, it is the brave confirmation of our uniqueness in our frailties, faults and countless imperfections as much as in our cravings, endeavours and dreams. As such, it is, of course, open to multiple interpretations.

Recalling Tony Blair's statement that 'this is the time to stick to our convictions and beliefs and make sure we do the right thing', leaves nonetheless nothing to recommend the 'right thing' for. The 'right thing' for him, quite idiorhythmic, was to disregard the views of those he was elected to represent, ignore the rule of law his country had pledged to defend in the UN, and, on the strength of totally unsubstantiated claims, launch an unprovoked attack against a country which could not even defend herself. Poet Yannis Ritsos was quite right when he said that 'we must rediscover the words and clean them' before using them again.

Associated with Reason, the 'right thing' is not the meeting of an obligation inherent in the intimidating structure of Kantian morality, a responsibility we have to assume or a debt we need to discharge. Nor is doing the 'right thing' the manifestation of a secretly pathological interest, an act of self-indulgence as Thomas Hobbes, the 'twin brother of fear', argued, which denies the act the meaning it represents, or a gesture due to calculation, conscious or unconscious, of restitution or reappropriation. The commitment is not, finally, impure in the sense that 'what a man's got to do' is not good in itself but good because it is, as the Greeks argued, in man's interest to do 'what he's got to do'. Until the time the thing good in itself gives a press conference to explain why it is good in itself without help from any justification external to it, a rational justification of goodness is the only one we can entertain. In any case, any external justification, in spite of its beaming smiles, can never be safe.

Besides, adventures in aetiology cannot be the excuse for moral neutrality and passive inactivity. Even if one's actions are interpreted as just another form of a dissimulated self-absorption, something pursued for one's own sake rather than the sake of the 'cause', the 'right thing' needs to be done. Justice, Democritus held, 'is doing what should be done, injustice not doing what should be done'. In this innocent Democritian form derived from Homer, doing 'the right thing' can never be an obligation if the commitment is not to deny itself, the cause for which it is made, and, finally, our own selves. It is a duty towards one's own rational self, which is probably the way Heracles saw things when asked by king Thespius to impregnate all his fifty daughters, which some claimed he did in a single night.

Rational judgment, intelligence, is critical in moral choices, indeed, a *sine qua non* condition, as the Greeks insisted. Character, which Aristotle said reveals 'moral purpose, showing what kind of things a man chooses or avoids', and intelligence cannot be separated. The Good life is not for the stupid, the unsculpted blocks of wood. A man cannot be both stupid and good as Christianity, and also Kant, held, for stupidity of a certain kind precludes goodness. *Pleonexia*, greed, and also *phthonos*, envy, two of the vices of the weak, are not just morally repulsive, they are also stupid. So is covetousness, arrogance, shamelessness or lust; and so are many other virtues to which the free market economy and its culture has given such an exalted rank. Hence Socrates' argument that all moral virtues were forms of knowledge. Virtue, he said, is knowledge, i.e., 'no-one errs willingly'. Intelligence includes practical intelligence on the understanding that man is good – practical intelligence without goodness is cunning, and cunning is not a virtue.

The context in which action takes place needs, of course, to be taken into account as some things are defined by the eternal law – that single universal common to all cases in tune with the natural order – but place, time, relation to other things, history, virtues, usefulness and substance define the context, different from one place to another and from one age to another. Though time has created a gap, the Greek perceptions are, however, still with us. When Findhorn Foundation ran a course on forgiveness, the underlying assumption was that unforgiveness is bad for us – not the unforgiven. The power of the ethical is still the power of Reason, but Reason as Logos, the voice of everything that is.

The Greeks' personal code of behaviour on which their gentlemen's world rested may be inaccessible by our commercial culture, but its main elements are easily recognisable, albeit only to be dismissed. Realism, never comfortable with ideas, would not make space for any other option. Still the Greek ethos is there, in the desperate calls for the building of character as opposed to personality and the pursuit of substance rather than image. It is in the invitation to become rather than simply be there as pathetic spectators of our own life, create rather than turn into the victims of consumption, identify with something bigger than the self and meet our destiny. It is also a reminder that our scarcely perceptible attempts to resist many of the demands of our culture, those abstruse impulses which are instantaneously suppressed, are perhaps the real thing, with all the rest being extraneous or delusive.

Man was inseparable from his destiny, the community, and in harmony with its objectives. The community was his home, his family, and had to be respected as much as the rights of the citizen and the individual had to be protected. Freedom was the citizen's birthright, democracy the system blessed by Mother Nature, and citizenship an honour. Arbitrary acts, the prerogative of the barbarians, could not be excused in cities of noblemen. The citizens had to refrain from criminal, unethical or even just indecorous acts, but more than that, committed to their community rather than to their own selves, they had also to make a positive contribution towards the welfare of their polis. Demonstrating with deeds the noble and generous side of their nature, wealthy citizens offered their support to, amongst others, the poor and the deserving. Nonetheless, few would seek the support of the community, for, in the proud Greek civilisation of honour, giving to, rather than receiving from, the right people, was the mark of the honourable man.

Those who failed to live up to the polis' expectations and violated the common trust were, even if they did nothing illegal, named and shamed. Letting down your friends, partners and fellow citizens, resorting to unethical practices or trespassing on the rights of the community for personal gain was contemptible. No individual rights could elbow out of existence the rights of the whole community. Naming and shaming had in those days to do with honour rather than the pursuit of dubious political objectives, which is what the most powerful Jewish lobby group in the US, the American-Israel Public Affairs Committee, did by naming those companies who were doing business with alleged state sponsors of terrorism.

Simplicity was the virtue only the unwise would not possess. Wealth was, likewise, dismissed because of its corrupting influence, and consumption was despicable. Drawing a line between man's limited 'natural' and his unlimited 'unnatural' needs, the Greek culture placed the emphasis on one's ability to control his appetites, curb his desires for material goods and focus, instead, on the development of his potentials. All citizens were in any case entitled, not just to equal rights before the law as in our own society, but to the enjoyment of everything their society considered to be good. On the other hand, inequality was accepted except that those with money had to spend it in a way beneficial to the community rather than for the satisfaction of lecherous pursuits.

Man, in any case, did not need much to live on – as in today's world, the best things in life cost no money. Having conquered their freedom from necessity, the necessity to work long hours to buy things they did not need, the Greeks were, thus, able to master their time and devote their energies to pursuits that filled their heart with happiness. The objective was personal growth, the attainment of *areté*, all the personal qualities that a man *kalos k' agathos* was associated with. These qualities required a presence in all fields – a man had to be a committed citizen, an honourable person, a creative thinker and a lover of beauty in all its forms, the beauty of the body and the mind, simplicity and self-restraint, nobility and courage. The understanding, totally alien to our own culture, even incompatible with it, was based on the notion of proportion, balance and symmetry leading, on the one hand, to the avoidance of excesses, and, on the other, to the all-rounded excellence of the individual.

As important was the Greek conviction that means are not means to an end, in our days the accumulation of wealth and power, but ends in themselves to be fully agreeable and enjoyable. No noble ends could, therefore, justify dishonourable means. Light years away from utilitarianism, things, likewise, had an intrinsic value for what they were rather than for the use they could be made of. The world was not out there to serve the interests of man, but to be lived in harmony with its purpose and its beauty. Golden-haired Harmony, created by the nine Muses of Pieria, was looking after it. Beauty and its pursuit was, indeed, the highest form of living, but beauty, as an aesthetic concept, embraced not just art but the whole way of being. It signified love of the beautiful, in its aesthetic, moral, intellectual and physical form as it manifested itself in a person's character, the culture of the time or the foreign policy of the state.

As opposed to the Christian culture of faith and the capitalist culture of profit, the Greek culture was the culture of joy to which the Romans did subscribe but only to orientalise it in due time just as modernism subscribed to the values of the Enlightenment only to vulgarise them in no time. Still this brilliant culture can only be a source of inspiration for us, for its basic tenets reside in our subconscious. Honour, courage, wisdom, simplicity, truthfulness, responsibility, self-restraint, kindness and *sophrosyne*, temperate thinking, the virtues a good man displays always in action, are all within reach.

Personal quality is manifested in the individual's determination to do the 'right thing' whatever the circumstances or the costs. Public statements can, therefore, only be as good as the way we live our lives. Statements are made not just by demonstrations, violent or otherwise, but also by the manifestation of personal quality, a prerequisite to both the smooth running of society and the *eudaemonia* of the individual. Vociferously attacking American hegemony in public may be necessary for the democratisation of the world order. It is, however, meaningless if the same person who opposes the world's domination by a great Power honours the concept of domination in his own home. Opposing the greed of the multinationals may, likewise, be the honourable course an individual can take. But it is inconsequential if the same person, always looking for more and better which is always a little further down the road, cannot control his own private appetites. And supporting the rights of the disadvantaged gives nobody the right to take advantage of the welfare state, make indeed a career out of it, and end up as a burden on the community. Freedoms are important, but they need to be filled with the meaning denied to them by the contemporary world.

Personally, I have confronted this issue many times to my utmost frustration and irritation. I have seen people committed to democracy, and paying at times an exorbitant price for it, only to betray their ideals because of their own control-freak inner selves. I have associated with others contributing generously to noble causes and yet eaten up by ambition, envy, selfishness, greed, intemperance, bitterness, callousness, negativity or pretension. I have also met socialists, arrogant, devoid of any human feelings, indifferent to pain unless pain can be translated into the language of ideology, people whom a modern Greek would call *fellós – fellós* means cork, and it describes a person without substance, someone who, if thrown into the sea, would float like a cork. Perhaps, just like Dostoevsky's Raskolnikov, we are all compelled by some inner drive constantly to betray ourselves.

In this sense blame for things going wrong cannot be placed at the door of politicians as they are no longer the children of a debased aristocracy or a pugnacious plutocracy. They are, instead, the offspring of middle class, even poor, families, whose values and culture they reflect. The responsibility belongs to the individual, who, abdicating it, is ready to abuse the system, if and when it suits or missuits his or her interests. Yet, somehow, we fail to see it. Instead, if I can take the modern Greeks as an example, we are always ready to blame anyone for our misfortunes – the British or Americans, preferably both, and their secret services, international capitalism, the government, the Turks, the Capricorns. Never ourselves. Varnalis, the old horse of a poetry fragrant and brusque as the blood of Dionysos, raised the issue in a few immortal lines. Whom can we blame, he wondered, 'our hoodoo karma, a loathing God, our loopy head or the wine?'

A truly meaningful outer change can never come if it depends on undependable individuals. It can only be brought about if it goes hand in hand with one's own inner transformation, or, as Aristotle insisted, with one's own elevated self, for only a changed person – a courageous person committed to fairness and honesty, a good friend to his friends and a contributing member of the community – can hold the promise of a better future. Though only too self-evident, this is hugely underrated, ignored, sometimes even contemptuously dismissed. Those pursuing structural changes, too full of self-importance, deal condescendingly with those on the path of inner transformation, whilst those engaged in inner work cannot often even grasp the importance of reaching out to what is commonly called reality. Yet without working at both levels, the inner and the outer, the personal and the political, the individual and his or her culture, the road to change will remain blocked. The 'good life', Aristotle said, is neither a life spent on the golf course nor in front of the television set, but a life committed to the pursuit of higher goals that help develop human potential in the context of the polis. In such a context, people reach their potential, like water does its level.

As if it is inscribed upon the ebony of the night, the Left will not, however, easily see this truth. Its drive is towards policy choices dictated by a sense of social justice, which nevertheless cannot be achieved in a society consisting of self-seeking individuals, full of themselves and as guilty for the unseemliness and tribulations of life as the system itself.

The realisation that the world is not only about the structures and institutions of the male, but also about our personal world with which the female, whether conditioned or not, feels much more at ease shifted something in me of fundamental importance. Like Odysseus, I moved on from the manly world of the Iliad, the early experiences of my childhood's heroic age, to the abstruse and person-centred muliebritous world of Odyssey and experienced the import of the female. The system was then understood, not only in terms of its foreign, economic or military policies, but also in terms of its often devastating effect on the lives of so many individuals and the latters' responsibility for it. This kind of understanding, which exists best in the haziness of abstraction before it finds its way to the precision of the final form, demands self-scanning in the active presence of the 'other mind', the unattended, undeveloped, even unacknowledged thinking of the female, indispensable if the male thinking focusing on structures and institutions is to be challenged.

Cambridge University Professor John Dunn reminded us of it in his book *The Cunning of Unreason*. 'If the purposes which govern state power ... are to become wiser, less myopic or more austere', he pointed out, 'it is we who must change, not the states to which we belong'. We should not, perhaps, live with the single expectation to be free to do what we want – a kind of *laissez-faire* for everybody. Freedom is not the independence of a free will, but the responsibility, indispensable to the community, with which one conducts oneself both in private and in the public domain. What matters here are the choices we make as individuals, and these choices are the product of our education and upbringing. This is what Adamantios Korais, the patriarchal figure of the Greek Enlightenment denounced by the Greek ecclesiastical authorities as an 'impious Hellen', had in mind when insisting that change is an educational process, which was his own version of the 'Long Revolution'.

Education in the Western world has reached its highest level ever, yet one cannot really expect to meet many such changed persons waiting in vain on the platform of Waterloo station for the train. Our culture, encouraging a passion for the ordinary, the Jeffrey Archer narrative, thriving on image rather than character, and valuing gratification rather than responsibility, discourages their emergence; and culture, as professor Zygmunt Baumann pointed out, is power, able to order, control and separate.

Hence, to follow Raymond Williams, culture as something referring to a whole way of life, material, intellectual and spiritual, is central to structures of change, control and democracy. Institutional change is never going to be far reaching as long as the culture does not change, and it is never going to be good enough if it does not reflect the transformation of the entire subjective form of life. People will never be involved in the running of their common affairs if nobody does anything, if he can help it, for anyone; and they will never contribute anything to the common good if all that matters is 'me'. Individualism, this perhaps incurable disease of our civilisation, has to give way to a healthy understanding of our common problems and shared interests, to kindness, grace, humility and generosity of spirit; and all subjective rights have to be matched by a sense of the individual's responsibility towards the whole. Liberals, objecting to the dandified individualism of our society, cannot ignore the input of the free market which is both generated by, and reproduces, an individualism ready to step over society's dead body.

Likewise, our ever-growing needs, ever-frustrated as we can never have the best others seem to enjoy, have to be reconsidered. Immoderate wealth benefits neither the world nor the individual. Even its very having, as Gabriel Marcel, the French Christian existentialist, pointed out, affects a person – he becomes anxious about it and instead of possessing it, he begins to be possessed by it. Everything in life is about natural limits which we cannot cross without inviting catastrophe. Life, with plenty of oil in its lamp, is more than possessions just as we are more than objects, things, commodities with a value fixed in line with the qualifications supplied by schooling. This may be self-evident – 'how can I see the world like this?', asks the Tao. 'Because I have eyes'. But the capacity of our world, a world whose ancestors are dead in our memories, to miss the obvious will never desert us, which is a good reason to go for some psychotherapy as long as psychotherapy does not interfere with our psyche and we can continue to enjoy without perturbation our opulent absurdities.

What is missing in this respect is not intelligence, but willingness to see the right and the good and act accordingly. 'The difficulty', Demosthenes said, 'is not in explaining to you what is best to do ... but in making you actually do it'. The beauty, in its moral sense, which obliterates the wall between self and the other, the personal and the impersonal, the particular and the general and makes life worth living gives way to self-interest. But mock beauty, as William Blake, the rebel against authority, would have said once again, and 'you throw the sand against the wind, and the wind blows it back again'.

Going back to the initial assumptions, we might discover what is engraved in our psyche. Letting free the imagination, which is threatened, South African author J M Coetzee said, by middle class security, we may then see again everything in the world as part of 'us', recognise the essential interdependence of everything that is, and accord it the respect it is entitled to on account of the divinity it confers upon itself. We might also see Justice, the foundation of the Greeks' secular society, as the religion of our own world, the bedrock of man's decency unfolded without fear of God or expectation of rewards in the afterlife, and trust again man's ability to reign over himself. It is in the spirit of man, the great Pericles said, that we place our trust – not systems, policies or much less kings or Gods. If faith in it withers, Sophocles tells us, falsehood blooms. Faith, of course, may not take us far, but its absence will take us nowhere.

Heading towards the call of Logos, rather than masters of nature or slaves of the Lord, we may be able to feel again an integral part of the world, free and yet committed to it as a condition of survival. We may re-establish Justice as the supreme moral law in tune with both our time's and the eternal moral norms, reconnect with the sense of balance, proportion and symmetry, and appreciate things for what they are rather than for their market value. We may, likewise, rediscover the joy of being rather than having, creating rather than consuming and living tastefully but simply as full human beings – sensual, intellectual, spiritual, communal. We may nurture our individuality, but in harmony with the interests of the community, seek happiness in doing 'the right thing', and find meaning in interaction with our world rather than in the mysteries of the beyond or the abyss of the self.

We may, finally, seek beauty as it manifests itself in a gentle smile, a kind word, a love affair, in the sparkling eyes of a child, the company of a friend, the whisper of the waves, in the workings of the mind, a person's character or the running of the state, and look afresh for inspiration in the transformation of our institutions and our lives. In a sane world, flowing as noiselessly as Alpheus, there is no room for extremes whether in the form of huge income inequalities, food fads, religious fundamentalism or repressive practices. The world, its humour, innocence, generosity, love, friendship, has something divine in itself, and its divinity is eager to be revealed in all its awe to anyone open to it, to cuddle us with its bodiless fingers and engulf us in the serenity of the intangible when we can identify with an essence that is beyond us: Justice, beauty, time, love, simplicity, rhythm, creativity, perfection, silence. It is there when matter and spirit merge in a way that creates new realities which reflect the totality of our existence, the infinitude of the self or the magic of the imperceptible.

The journey to the distant shores of the unknown, to the forbidden sunlight, to all the things which 'cannot be permitted to be true', is, of course, resisted by the known. Reluctant to succumb to the charms of a misty dream, reality will never let us search for a visionary consciousness, return to the primal innocence and goodness of the

Golden Age, 'freed', as Pierre Bonnard, the anarchist, said, 'from the order of time'. With all the pleasure of a man who is forced to displease, so will all those concerned about means and ends, the pragmatist and the utilitarian, or the pessimist for whom things are already bad enough to need improvements. We can expect nothing else, either, from habit, our worst enemy to which we have pledged our loyalty – habit will just dismiss the dream as an irksome deviation from a flavourless existence, unfrequented by passions, the feckless quest for the Holy Grail. But the journey is not a pilgrimage or, as poet Manolis Anagnostakis would have it, 'a trip somewhere, out of boredom I suppose, or to be able to say that we too have been places'.

It is, instead, a personal revolution for the liberation from the concentration camp in which madness has confined our minds. The revolution needs to be made, for although there are powers which we cannot resist, we do not have to surrender to them. Many, of course, do, the fugitives from the land of fortitude. This cannot, however, be the choice of the free human being, the person who values life.

For, if 'nothing moves you much but your own plight', as poet James Reeves put it so daintily, you might as well 'close the book and say good-night'.

Part V: Epilogue

The Education of Desire

The dream of a better world, a vital feature of the unconscious landscape, is anything but a pathetic fantasy offered with complimentary drinks by the muddled. A dream is reality, another form of reality, which challenges, surpasses and overrides the reality of the senses, the alternative which has the power to inspire, motivate and activate. That was the case with Martin Luther King's 'I have a dream that my four little children will one day live in a nation where they will be judged not by the colour of their skin but by the content of their character'. His emancipatory vision and its underlying spiritual message, which, to borrow a line from Rita Boumi-Pappas' poetry, turns the 'veins into rivers that irrigate fields of rapture', galvanised millions into action and dramatically changed the American social landscape.

In a secular society, unwilling to be galvanised by visions of life after death, the dream, the image of everything with blood in its veins, is the signpost indicating the ideal as articulated by the emotionally and spiritually fulfilling direction we might want to follow. It is, as E.P. Thompson, the social historian, said, the 'education of desire' which 'opens the way to aspiration', or the 'cultivation of the soul', the term Cicero used to describe the purpose of philosophy. It is also the means of confronting a hostile world by remaking it in the image of our desires, engaging for the purpose society's critical faculties and developing the creative thinking of its members. Utopian ideas, Karl Mannheim, the Hungarian-born German sociologist, said, are 'not ideologies', but 'orientations' which can 'shatter, either partially or wholly, the order of things prevailing at the time'.

Utopianism, the undefined arena in which 'the attainable and the unattainable meet and look curiously at one another', is not concerned with practicalities. It embraces, instead, the unthinkable which rekindles the fire within and acuminates the capacity for wonder blunted by the survival skills' textbook we have all learnt by heart. 'Be a realist, demand the impossible', the inspiration behind the movement of May '68, is anything but as absurd as it sounds. It is not all that new, either – Ovid's *nitimur in vetutum*, we strive after the forbidden, what is placed beyond our reach, had a not dissimilar ring. The boundaries of the dream, though we contain them, are, therefore, next to impossible to determine. Hence, travelling in the direction of our hopes, towards what Nietzsche called 'the ocean of the soul's goal', we need to be prepared to sail outside culture's perimeters, round the curves of time, into the sparkling marvels of the intimidating unknown, depending, in order not to be lost, on our instinctual courage and on our own sense of direction.

The dream is, of course, as weak as the weakest argument in its favour. Yet its presence is the assertion of the positive over the negative, the individual's expression of solidarity with mankind, a vote of self-confidence which re-energises and sustains our belief in ourselves and holds us together in the pursuit of the common good. On it rests the prospect of a meaningful individual existence and the community's will to live. As such, it is a breath of fresh air in the gloomy, sultry room in which our lives, 'reprehensibly perfect', go 'unspent', a ray of sunlight breaking through the heavy black smoke of burnt seductive promises.

Utopia, in this sense, although it does not provide 'recipes for the cookshops of the future', as Marx of all people noted, is an educator. Maintaining the tension between reality and ideal, between the 'I am' and the 'I ought', it relativises the present and de-legitimises its claims. It provides, as Plato put it, a standard against which we can judge the situation we are in, and stands up against the passive surrender of the individual to the madness of a disequilibrated world. As such, it is the refusal to concede to instrumental Reason its intellectual claims, a statement against the defeatism, cynicism and resignation of our times, a challenge to the status quo and its structure of feelings. Rather than be concerned about the future, which is what it is often associated with, Utopia is, instead, a critical assessment of the present as seen from a distance, the evaluation of current realities by the non-ephemeral, a different perspective which helps us to rethink life, explore alternatives and inform our choices. Thinking is in any case what we need to do. The 'unexamined life', as Socrates held, is 'not worth living'. Even if it did not exist, Utopia would have to be invented.

Of course, we all know that Utopia, the dream that cannot be documented, holds no promises. One may even argue that there is nothing really to dream about. People, as Goethe said, could become cleverer and more penetrating, but neither better nor happier. After all, as all of us traumatised by innocence know, perfection is out of reach, and suffering, even if science and technology can help the sensitive with soul transplants, will never end. At least death, illness and old age, or to use R.D. Laing's term 'ontological insecurity', guarantee it. So does the dark, the distempered side of human nature, or the unflattering references to ourselves by all those miserable people who have everything but taste. Whatever we do, the obstacles to the fulfilment of our expectations seem bound to be there; and the sweet hour of joy and love, if and when it comes, can be expected to last no longer than an orgasm.

But the Utopian impulse is in our nature: we cannot do without a vision of a future in which our desires, fantasies, cravings and wishes for a better world, sometimes unconscious, are met, as we cannot live without hope. The unfolding of new and enthralling possibilities, as many as the imagination can produce, is what gives life its substance and direction – 'I was alone with all that could happen', Jorge, anything but alone, utters in ecstasy in William Gass's story *The Pedersen Kid*. Often we are, of course, confronted by forces beyond our control, and we never know what is going to happen next. Yet we can never stop. The attainment of human perfection is a never-ending job. Hence, as Socrates concluded between glasses of retsina albeit watered down, and happy, I presume, to say so again, 'satisfied with himself', can be 'only he who is neither good nor wise'. Urbanski, the fellow who, in Henry Miller's *The Colossus of Marousi*, had gone one winter's night to a bordel in Montreal to emerge from it in spring, will, I suspect, have a different opinion.

Utopianism, just like the era in which we could understand how the things we used worked, has been out of fashion for a generation. But the Utopian impulse, which in dispiriting moments one may wish had a body to be sent for good to Guantánamo Bay as an enemy combatant, has anything but disappeared. It has been there with all the power of its fragility embodying our aspirations rather than our fears, our hopes rather than our despair, and our love rather than our hatred. 'Warily, self-questioningly, and setting its own limits', as Raymond Williams put it, it has been renewing itself in confrontation with social injustices, corruption and war. It is being reaffirmed in the struggle against a society 'normless, self-centred, and driven by greed, special interests, and an unabashed quest for power'.

'Abstract' or 'systemic' Utopias, founded on universal visions with an intrinsic quality and definable boundaries and promoted by those which Anna Akhmatova, the Russian dissident poet, referring in particular to the Stalinists, called 'experts in the manufacture of orphans', are no longer attractive. They were used as instruments of repression and control, and were decidedly rejected at least by the Western intellectual élite, which no longer seeks the 'truth', the light. 'Perhaps', as Kavafis, the poet, put it, 'the light will be a new tyranny. Who knows what new things it will show'. The universal answers to the problems of the age sought by born-again Christian president George W. Bush, his free market apostles and his military crusaders at the beginning of the new millennium has just confirmed their undesirability. So has the revival of monolithic fundamentalism.

At least in the West new forms have emerged, 'concrete' Utopias, those, in other words, which, taking the usual feminine precautions, do not drink and drive. The 'concrete' is Utopianism as function, the venture beyond the given which 'disrupts the taken-for-granted nature of the present'. As Raymond Williams held, the only option is a heuristic Utopia which, relying on the strength of its vision, searches for alternative values, allows scope for the 'education of desire', and challenges both the omnipotent power of the market and its repressive religious critics.

Though we are determined by a lot of things, we also have some choice, particularly in issues involving moral and ethical responsibility in both interpersonal relations and the way we deal with the world. Choices can be negotiated in the individual's consciousness, and the individual can distance himself from what Nietzsche called 'the herd' with its mediocre values. He or she, with an imperceptible force, can strive for the attainment of the higher goals of both humanity and self. In doing so, in harmony with the commands of his better self, and indifferent to the sufferings a principled position is bound to engender, man may be able to distil his essence and achieve oneness with his truth. It is what will enable him to dream again.

But this takes courage, the courage of conviction that often goes together with self-denial. For Christians, this is the way to reconcile man and God. For atheists, it is the way to reconcile man and the world and ensure that Justice does not disappear as a virtue. This courage has not been missing despite the fact that a whole generation in the last quarter of the twentieth century displayed the same interest in grand visions as a turkey in Greek irregular verbs. Right action, not as a means to an end, but as an end in itself, seems sometimes to be a virtue that Sisyphus would hardly make a commitment to in exchange for his punishment. It requires a commitment to martyrdom.

But a career as a martyr currently has no openings. Breakfast with heroes is altogether out of fashion. Nevertheless, as the Romans used to say, *Dum spiro, spero.*

Index

Ackerman, prof. Bruce 34
Adorno, Theodor 6, 34, 43
Aeschylus 39
Agamemnon 39
Agathon 84
Akhmatova, Anna 175
Alban, Saint 61
Althusser, Louis 42
Amphilochus 142
Anagnostakis, Manolis 171
Annan, Kofi 129
Archer, Jeffrey 168
Arendt, Hannah 18, 38, 48, 51
Aristotle 14, 31, 36, 44, 49, 50, 88, 136, 144, 151, 153, 159, 161, 166
Armani, Giorgio 99
Arnold, Matthew 50
Arthur, King 61
Athanasiou, Tom 90
Atwood, Margaret 46
Augustine, Saint 29
Austen, Jane 78, 146
Axelos, Costas 137, 139-40
Ayer, A.J. 24

Bacon, Francis 61
Bacon, Roger 61
Bahro, Rudolf 88, 90, 141
Bailey, Alice 56-7, 59, 60-1, 64-5
Baudrillard, Jean 52
Baumann, Zygmunt 168
Beckham, David 99
Beethoven, Ludwig Van 10, 14
Bellerophon 20
Bentham, Jeremy 26
Bergson, Henri 155
Berlin, Isaiah 48
Berlusconi, Silvio 96, 121
Bernays, Edward 110
Bernstein, Eduard 33
Berry, Wendell 86
Bertalanffy, Ludwig von 58
Black, Conrad 121
Blair, Tony 5, 21, 30, 43, 73, 92, 96, 105, 116, 130, 169
Blake, William 14, 169
Blavatsky, Helena 57, 59, 61-5
Bloch, Ernst 137
Bloom, William 60, 67
Blunkett, David 147
Bodhidharma, Buddhist Patriarch 59
Bonnard, Pierre 171
Bookchin, Murray 15, 34, 62, 88, 137, 141
Boumi-Pappas, Rita 172
Bourdieu, Pierre 137
Brecht, Bertolt 84
Broch, Herman 13
Brontë, Charlotte 28
Brooke, Rupert 74
Brown, Gordon 130
Buber, Martin 35
Buffett, Warren 100

Bush, George W. 21, 120, 152, 175
Butler, Judith 78
Byron, George Gordon, Lord 5, 14, 63, 144

Cage, Nicholas 85
Calasso, Roberto 13
Callicles 26
Cambronne, Marshal 85
Cameron, David 110
Campbell, Joseph 65
Camus, Albert 44-6
Capra, Fritjof 58
Castoriades, Cornelius 38, 137
Castro, Fidel 107
Causley, Charles 64
Ching, Tao Te 63-4, 169
Chomsky, Noam 36, 96
Chopra, Deepak 65-6, 68
Chrysippus 68
Chrysostom, John 61
Cicero, Marcus Tullius 172
Clinton, Bill 92
Clinton, Hillary 39
Coetzee, J.M. 169
Coleridge, Samuel Taylor 14, 153
Columbus, Christopher 67, 112
Conche, Marcel 8
Count St Germain 61
Crittenden, Danielle 78
Crosland, Anthony 153

Dahl, Robert 115
Darwin, Charles 36
Davidson, Gordon 66-7
De Saussure, Ferdinand 42
Delacroix, Eugène 44
Democritus 39, 50, 159, 161
Demosthenes 23, 113, 123, 174
Derrida, Jacques 42, 127
Dickens, Charles 26
Diogenes 17
Dostoevsky, Fyodor 165
Douglas, Michael 85, 99
Dunn, John 167
Durkheim, Émile 42, 132
Dworkin, Ronald 23, 34, 133, 154
Dyer, Wayne 66

Eckhart, Johannes 87
Eco, Umberto 63
Eichmann, Adolf 30
El Greco 36
Eliot, T.S. 53, 158
Elytis, Odysseus 95, 150
Emerson, Ralph Waldo 9
Empedocles 37
Empson, William 95
Erdoe, Monsignor Peter 127
Escriva, Josemaria 104
Etzioni, Amitai 91-2
Euripides 75, 132

Ferguson, Sarah 69
Feuerbach, Ludwig Andreas 16

Fishkin, James 94
Flaubert, Gustave 42
Foot, Philippa 48
Fotopoulos, Takis 130
Foucault, Michel 7, 42
Fourier, Joseph 129
Fowles, John 156
Francis of Assisi, Saint 91
Frankel, Boris 91
Franklin, Benjamin 27
Frederick William II of Prussia 15
Freedman, Milton 93
Freud, Sigmund 40, 42, 110, 112, 142, 158
Fromm, Erich 46, 140, 158-9
Fukuyama, Francis 148
Furman, Ashrita 24

Gandhi, Mahatma 70
Gass, William 174
Gates, Bill 100
Gauguin, Paul 94
Gellner, Ernest 21
Gibbon, Edward 5
Gide, André 95
Giovanni, Don 157
Giraudoux, Jean 108
Goethe, Johann Wolfgang von 11, 13-4, 174
Goffman, Erving 27
Goldmann, Lucien 138
Gorgophone 22
Gorz, André 81, 89

Gramsci, Antonio 54, 137, 145
Grass, Günter 53, 95
Greer, Germaine 74, 80
Griffey, Harriet 41
Guevara, Ché 70
Guha, Ramachandra 111
Gurdjieff, George Ivanovitch 56
Gutierrez, Alberto Diaz 70
Gyges 37

Habermas, Jürgen 7, 34-5, 42, 102, 116, 127, 137, 141, 148
Hare, Richard Mervyn 34
Hay, Louise 68
Hayek, Friedrich 154
Hegel, Georg W.F. 11, 16, 32, 81
Heidegger, Martin 10, 15, 18, 44-5, 89, 151
Heracles 26, 161
Heraclitus 16, 51, 142, 155-6
Herodotus 19, 21
Hesiod 142
Hess, Rudolf 87
Hitler, Adolf 30, 61
Hobbes, Thomas 27, 42, 48, 160
Hölderlin, Friedrich 14
Homer 161
Horace 111
Horkheimer, Max 6
Horney, Karen 7
Humboldt, Wilhelm von 13, 50

Hume, David 42, 48-9
Huxley, Aldous 34, 50

Ibsen, Henrik 95
Ignatieff, Michael 134
Illich, Ivan 34, 89
Irigaray, Luce 42, 73, 76-7

Jackson, Michael 23
James, William 42, 45
Jaspers, Karl 35, 44, 48
John Paul II, Pope 46, 104
Johnson, Lyndon 96
Johnson, Samuel 37
Jolie, Angelina 99
Jong, Erica 77
Jospin, Lionel 114
Joyce, James 137
Jung, Carl 56-7, 59, 64, 68

Kafka, Franz 42
Kalvos, Andreas 108, 131
Kant, Immanuel 15, 16, 29, 31-3, 48-9
Kautsky, Karl 33
Kavafis, Konstantinos 176
Kazantzakis, Nicos 5, 18, 53
Kellner, Douglas 84
Khul, Djwhal, the Tibetan 64
Kierkegaard, Søren 32
King, Martin Luther 70, 173
Kingsolver, Barbara 123
Kipling, Rudyard 87
Kondylis, Panajotis 134, 140

Korais, Adamantios 167
Korf, Christian von 60
Kouchner, Bernard 98
Krishnamurti, Jiddu 63-5
Kristeva, Julia 75
Kropotkin, Peter 91, 96
Kundera, Milan 18-9
Kustow, Michael 9
Kymlicka, Will 94, 133

Lacan, Jacques 42, 158
Laing, R.D. 174
Lambert, Shaena 20
Larkin, Philip 5
Lawrence, D.H. 35, 42, 140
Le Doeuff, Michele 77
Lefebvre, Henri 137, 139
Leivaditis, Tasos 71
Lennon, John 148
Levi, Primo 54
Lorca, Federico Garcia 65
Lovelock, James 58, 86
Luhmann, Niklas 102
Lukács, Georg 42, 137-8
Luther 29
Luther, Martin 70, 172
Lyotard, Jean-François 146

MacIntyre, Alasdair 27, 37
Madonna 52
Mandelson, Peter 62
Mannheim, Karl 50, 156, 172
Marcel, Gabriel 35, 44, 168
Marcuse, Herbert 10, 18, 42,

69, 137, 141
Martial 28, 146
Martin, Ricky 99
Marx, Karl 10, 11, 16, 32-3, 42, 137-40, 151, 154, 173
Maslow, Abraham 49, 51, 140
Matisse, Henrí 13
McLaughlin, Corinne 66-7
Menander 39
Menelaus 72
Merkel, Angela 127
Merleau- Ponty, Maurice 140
Michelman, prof. Frank 34
Mill, John Stuart 26
Miller, Henry 174
Mitroff, Ian 70
Moore, Deni 73
Moore, G.E. 24, 26, 48
Mopsus 142
Moravia, Alberto 40
Morris, William 50, 72, 91
Moss, Kate 55
Mouzelis, Nicos 97
Murdoch, Iris 23
Murdoch, Rupert 116
Mussolini, Benito 7
Myrivilis, Stratis 158

Neill, Fiona 78
Nero, Emperor 20
Neruda, Pablo 39
Neville, Jill 76
Nietzsche, Friedrich 10, 11, 14, 16-7, 24, 27, 32, 34, 42, 173, 176
Nisbet, Robert 90
North Whitehead, Alfred 9
Nozick, Robert 114, 154

Odysseus 25-6, 167
Ovid 172
Owen, Robert 42, 129

Palladas 156
Pamuk, Orhan 158
Pareto, Vilfredo 7
Pascal, Blaise 22
Pasolini, Pier Paolo 149
Patanjali, Hindu 58
Pateman, Carole 74, 79
Pearson, Alison 78
Peck, M. Scott 59
Pericles 43, 169
Perseus 22
Phaon 13
Phillips, Melanie 77-8
Piaget, Jean 138
Plato 15, 27, 29, 50, 81, 121, 134, 155, 159, 173
Plethon, Gemistos 16
Plotinus 6, 57, 59, 60
Podaleirius 152
Polycrates 100
Porphyry 156
Poulantzas, Nicos 42, 115
Pound, Ezra 10
Proclus 61
Prometheus 71

Protagoras 44
Proulx, E. Annie 76
Proust, Marcel 13
Putnam, Robert 93

Rabin, Yitzak 22
Rawls, John 23, 26, 33, 133, 151, 153
Reagan, Ronald 93, 114, 153
Reeves, Donald 67
Reeves, James 171
Reich, Wilhelm 137, 158
Rilke, Rainer Maria 11, 17, 81
Ritsos, Yannis 13, 161
Roberts, Julia 36
Roberts, Michèle 79
Rogers, Carl 140
Roszak, Theodore 90
Rousseau, Jean-Jacques 42-3, 49, 77
Royal, Ségolène 94
Rubel, Maximilien 138
Rushdie, Salman 69-70, 136
Ruskin, John 153
Russell, Bertrand 10, 53, 66, 68
Ryle, Bishop 14
Sale, Kirkpatrick 90
Samuel, the prophet 61
Sappho 13
Sarkozy, Nicolas 13, 98
Saro-Wiwa, Ken 105
Sartre, Jean-Paul 32, 44-8, 140
Scheler, Max 34
Schiller, Friedrich 11, 13

Schumacher, Fritz 90
Seferis, George 35, 72
Segius 146
Sennett, Richard 155
Shakespeare, William 10, 61, 72
Sheldrake Rupert 58
Shelley, Mary 43
Shelley, Percy Bysshe 6, 9-10, 12, 14
Showalter, Elaine 77
Shriver, Lionel 78
Simmel, Georg 34, 131
Sisyphus 20, 45, 176
Skocpol, Theda 115
Smart, J.J.C. 28
Smiley, Jane 72
Smith, Adam 113
Smith, Joan 13
Socrates 8, 9, 22, 27, 30, 53, 139, 161, 173-4
Sophocles 25-6, 139, 169
Soros, George 91
Southey, Robert 14
Spezzano, Chuck 66
Stein, Edith 104
Steiner, Rudolf 87
Stevenson, Francis 26
Swift, Jonathan 64

Tallis, Raymond 146
Tawney, R.H. 35, 144, 154
Taylor, Charles 29, 132
Teresa, Mother 65

Thackeray, William Makepeace 154
Thales 47
Thatcher, Margaret 114, 153
Thespius, King 161
Thompson, E.P. 137, 172
Thrasymachus 26, 149
Thucydides 51
Tillich, Paul 44, 49
Tolstoy, Leo 35-6
Tocqueville, Alexis de 135

Updike, John 44

Veblen, Thorstein 34
Wagner, Richard 10
Walpole, Horace 54
Walter, Natasha 77
Weber, Max 6, 18, 34
Weeks, Jeffrey 83
Weldon, Fay 73
Wells, H.G. 127
Wenders, Wim 127
West, Cornel 102
Williams, Raymond 137, 153, 168, 176
Williams, Robbie 99
Winckelmann, J.J. 13
Wittgenstein, Ludwig 24, 50
Wolf, Naomi 80
Wolfensohn, James 147
Wolff, F.G.A. 13
Wollstonecraft, Mary 77
Wordsworth, William 14, 73, 149

Yeats, W.B. 19, 56, 96
Zarathustra 17

Zemurray, Sam 'the Banana Man' 106

YANNIS ANDROCOPOULOS: THE SKYROS TRILOGY

In Bed With Madness: Trying to make sense in a world that doesn't *by Yannis Androcopoulos*

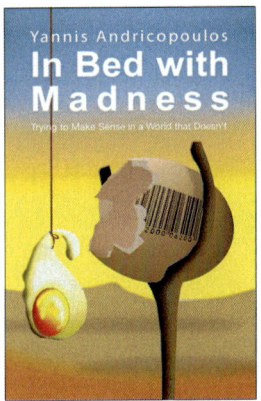

Globalism endowed us with McDonald's, 'the world's local bank', English football teams without English players and an irrepressible desire for more as enough is never good enough – the blanket is always too short. Our personal world as much as our social and political realities seem to have blithely surrendered to the madness of a civilization which views anything from corporate greed and global warming to military adventures and religious fundamentalism as normal as a door banging in the wind. The destructive capabilities of our age have run too far ahead of our wisdom. However, the process is not irreversible if our thinking can postpone its retirement. *In Bed with Madness* is 'a well-argued, powerful and profound indictment of contemporary culture', stylishly written – a reviewer said he would have bought it just for its humour!

200 pp., £8.95 / $17.90, 978-1845401290 (pbk.)

The Greek Inheritance: Ancient Greek wisdom for the digital era *by Yannis Androcopoulos*

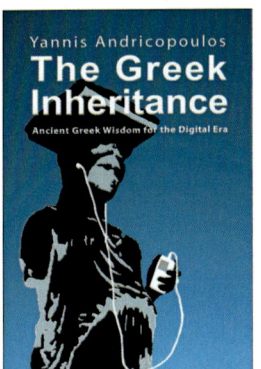

The culture of ancient Greece, a culture of joy, was replaced by the Judaeo-Christian culture of faith and then by the capitalist culture of profit. Yet it is the only culture worth fighting for if we want a world run by humans rather than theocracies, nanotechnologies or private equity funds. Yannis Andricopoulos views the Greek culture as the front line of the battle against individualism, materialism, authoritarianism and religious extremism. In a world turned into the corporations' playground, this is also the battle for human values, civic virtues and an ethical society. *The Greek Inheritance* traces the conflict between Greek values and those of the repressive, religious or capitalist order throughout the millennia. The book is challenging and well-written with a light, humorous touch.

260 pp., £8.95 / $17.90, 978-1845401306 (pbk.)

The Future of the Past: From the culture of profit to the culture of joy *by Yannis Androcopoulos*

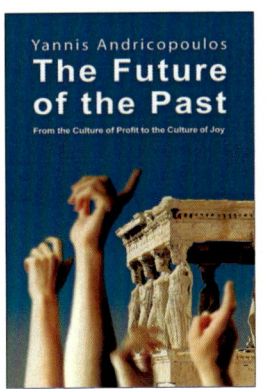

Universalism in its old forms has, just like door-to-door milkmen, gone for good. But the search for some universally accepted ethical standards cannot be abandoned – values are not colourless as the wind and odourless as thoughts. Looking into our world from the classical Greek point of view, Yannis Andricopoulos wonders whether we cannot place Justice again at the heart of our morality, look forward to the happiness of the individual rather than the upgrading of his or her consumer fantasies, and endeavour to create, not more wealth, but a just and honourable world. *The Future of the Past* is written in 'a lively, challenging style guaranteeing to stimulate debate on the most pressing issues of our time'.

Yannis Androcopoulos Ph.D, co-founder of Skyros holidays, is a former political journalist and editor of i-to-i magazine.

200 pp., £8.95 / $17.90, 978-1845401313 (pbk.)

Imprint Academic, PO Box 200, Exeter, EX5 5HE, UK   Tel: +44 (0)1392 851550
imprint-academic.com/skyros

Yannis Andricopoulos was born in Athens where he spent the formative years of his life – years scarred by wars, deprivation and political repression. 'We managed to survive', he says, 'but only on grains of hope.'

In 1964 he entered journalism with *Avghi*, an Athens daily, and in 1967 arrived in swinging London as his newspaper's correspondent. The happy event was, however, shortlived, for the Greek military dictatorship (1967-1974) deprived him of his nationality. His actions, the colonels claimed, 'were detrimental to the interests of Greece'. Forced to stay in the UK as a political refugee, he completed a Ph.D. in Diplomatic History at Birkbeck College, University of London, and also headed the Greek National Union of Students in exile (1969-1971). The latter's activities caused his expulsion from three East European countries.

In 1974, when the military regime collapsed, he resumed his career as London-based foreign correspondent first for *Avghi* and later for *Eleftherotypia*, another Athens daily. In the same year he published his first book in Athens, an edited version of prime minister Churchill's personal papers on 1944 Greece. As a historian he has since published another three books on 20th century Greek and European history and as a journalist he has reported from various troublespots in the world. On meeting prime minister Margaret Thatcher at 10 Downing Street, unable all of a sudden to work out whether she was a prime minister or a prime ministress, he could not open his mouth. Thankfully, she saved him with her kindness.

In 1979 he co-founded *Skyros*, the holistic community-based holiday centre on the Greek island of Skyros, which he still co-directs, and ten years later, from 1989 to 1994, was also the editor of *i-to-i* magazine, an alternative London publication. He is still a Greek citizen because, he says, he wants to cheer for Greece without feeling guilty when Greece plays against England. He now lives in the Isle of Wight where he co-founded *The Grange*, a small seaside centre offering various personal development courses.

The three books of this series have been inspired by both his involvement in the truculent world of politics and the graceful, personal world of Skyros.